# KWAME NKRUMAH

# KWAME NKRUMAH

Douglas Kellner

CHELSEA HOUSE PUBLISHERS
NEW YORK
NEW HAVEN     PHILADELPHIA

EDITOR-IN-CHIEF: Nancy Toff
EXECUTIVE EDITOR: Remmel T. Nunn
MANAGING EDITOR: Karyn Gullen Browne
COPY CHIEF: Perry Scott King
ART DIRECTOR: Giannella Garrett
PICTURE EDITOR: Elizabeth Terhune

*Staff for* KWAME NKRUMAH:

SENIOR EDITOR: John W. Selfridge
ASSISTANT EDITORS: Maria Behan, Pierre Hauser, Kathleen McDermott, Bert Yaeger
COPY EDITORS: Gillian Bucky, Sean Dolan
DESIGN ASSISTANT: Jill Goldreyer
PICTURE RESEARCH: Diane Wallis
LAYOUT: Debby Jay
PRODUCTION COORDINATOR: Alma Rodriguez
PRODUCTION ASSISTANT: Karen Dreste
COVER ILLUSTRATION: Jack Freas

CREATIVE DIRECTOR: Harold Steinberg


3  5  7  9  8  6  4  2

Frontispiece courtesy of The Bettmann Archive

Library of Congress Cataloging in Publication Data

Kellner, Douglas. KWAME NKRUMAH

(World leaders past & present)
Bibliography: p.
Includes index.
1. Nkrumah, Kwame, 1909–1972—Juvenile literature.
2. Ghana—Presidents—Biography—Juvenile literature.
3. Ghana—Politics and government—To 1957—Juvenile
literature. 4. Ghana—Politics and government—1957–1979—
Juvenile literature. [1. Nkrumah, Kwame, 1909–1972.
2. Presidents. 3. Ghana—Politics and government]
I. Title.  II. Series.
DT512.3.N57K45     1987     966.7'05'0924 [B] [92]       86-31681

ISBN 0-87754-546-4

# Contents

# C H E L S E A   H O U S E   P U B L I S H E R S

## W O R L D   L E A D E R S   P A S T   &   P R E S E N T

ADENAUER
ALEXANDER THE GREAT
MARC ANTONY
KING ARTHUR
ATATÜRK
ATTLEE
BEGIN
BEN-GURION
BISMARCK
LÉON BLUM
BOLÍVAR
CESARE BORGIA
BRANDT
BREZHNEV
CAESAR
CALVIN
CASTRO
CATHERINE THE GREAT
CHARLEMAGNE
CHIANG KAI-SHEK
CHURCHILL
CLEMENCEAU
CLEOPATRA
CORTÉS
CROMWELL
DANTON
DE GAULLE
DE VALERA
DISRAELI
EISENHOWER
ELEANOR OF AQUITAINE
QUEEN ELIZABETH I
FERDINAND AND ISABELLA
FRANCO

FREDERICK THE GREAT
INDIRA GANDHI
MOHANDAS GANDHI
GARIBALDI
GENGHIS KHAN
GLADSTONE
GORBACHEV
HAMMARSKJÖLD
HENRY VIII
HENRY OF NAVARRE
HINDENBURG
HITLER
HO CHI MINH
HUSSEIN
IVAN THE TERRIBLE
ANDREW JACKSON
JEFFERSON
JOAN OF ARC
POPE JOHN XXIII
LYNDON JOHNSON
JUÁREZ
JOHN F. KENNEDY
KENYATTA
KHOMEINI
KHRUSHCHEV
MARTIN LUTHER KING, JR.
KISSINGER
LENIN
LINCOLN
LLOYD GEORGE
LOUIS XIV
LUTHER
JUDAS MACCABEUS
MAO ZEDONG

MARY, QUEEN OF SCOTS
GOLDA MEIR
METTERNICH
MUSSOLINI
NAPOLEON
NASSER
NEHRU
NERO
NICHOLAS II
NIXON
NKRUMAH
PERICLES
PERÓN
QADDAFI
ROBESPIERRE
ELEANOR ROOSEVELT
FRANKLIN D. ROOSEVELT
THEODORE ROOSEVELT
SADAT
STALIN
SUN YAT-SEN
TAMERLANE
THATCHER
TITO
TROTSKY
TRUDEAU
TRUMAN
VICTORIA
WASHINGTON
WEIZMANN
WOODROW WILSON
XERXES
ZHOU ENLAI

# ON LEADERSHIP
## Arthur M. Schlesinger, jr.

LEADERSHIP, it may be said, is really what makes the world go round. Love no doubt smooths the passage; but love is a private transaction between consenting adults. Leadership is a public transaction with history. The idea of leadership affirms the capacity of individuals to move, inspire, and mobilize masses of people so that they act together in pursuit of an end. Sometimes leadership serves good purposes, sometimes bad; but whether the end is benign or evil, great leaders are those men and women who leave their personal stamp on history.

Now, the very concept of leadership implies the proposition that individuals can make a difference. This proposition has never been universally accepted. From classical times to the present day, eminent thinkers have regarded individuals as no more than the agents and pawns of larger forces, whether the gods and goddesses of the ancient world or, in the modern era, race, class, nation, the dialectic, the will of the people, the spirit of the times, history itself. Against such forces, the individual dwindles into insignificance.

So contends the thesis of historical determinism. Tolstoy's great novel *War and Peace* offers a famous statement of the case. Why, Tolstoy asked, did millions of men in the Napoleonic wars, denying their human feelings and their common sense, move back and forth across Europe slaughtering their fellows? "The war," Tolstoy answered, "was bound to happen simply because it was bound to happen." All prior history predetermined it. As for leaders, they, Tolstoy said, "are but the labels that serve to give a name to an end and, like labels, they have the least possible connection with the event." The greater the leader, "the more conspicuous the inevitability and the predestination of every act he commits." The leader, said Tolstoy, is "the slave of history."

Determinism takes many forms. Marxism is the determinism of class. Nazism the determinism of race. But the idea of men and women as the slaves of history runs athwart the deepest human instincts. Rigid determinism abolishes the idea of human freedom—

the assumption of free choice that underlies every move we make, every word we speak, every thought we think. It abolishes the idea of human responsibility, since it is manifestly unfair to reward or punish people for actions that are by definition beyond their control. No one can live consistently by any deterministic creed. The Marxist states prove this themselves by their extreme susceptibility to the cult of leadership.

More than that, history refutes the idea that individuals make no difference. In December 1931 a British politician crossing Park Avenue in New York City between 76th and 77th Streets around 10:30 P.M. looked in the wrong direction and was knocked down by an automobile—a moment, he later recalled, of a man aghast, a world aglare: "I do not understand why I was not broken like an eggshell or squashed like a gooseberry." Fourteen months later an American politician, sitting in an open car in Miami, Florida, was fired on by an assassin; the man beside him was hit. Those who believe that individuals make no difference to history might well ponder whether the next two decades would have been the same had Mario Constasino's car killed Winston Churchill in 1931 and Giuseppe Zangara's bullet killed Franklin Roosevelt in 1933. Suppose, in addition, that Adolf Hitler had been killed in the street fighting during the Munich *Putsch* of 1923 and that Lenin had died of typhus during World War I. What would the 20th century be like now?

For better or for worse, individuals do make a difference. "The notion that a people can run itself and its affairs anonymously," wrote the philosopher William James, "is now well known to be the silliest of absurdities. Mankind does nothing save through initiatives on the part of inventors, great or small, and imitation by the rest of us—these are the sole factors in human progress. Individuals of genius show the way, and set the patterns, which common people then adopt and follow."

Leadership, James suggests, means leadership in thought as well as in action. In the long run, leaders in thought may well make the greater difference to the world. But, as Woodrow Wilson once said, "Those only are leaders of men, in the general eye, who lead in action. . . . It is at their hands that new thought gets its translation into the crude language of deeds." Leaders in thought often invent in solitude and obscurity, leaving to later generations the tasks of imitation. Leaders in action—the leaders portrayed in this series—have to be effective in their own time.

And they cannot be effective by themselves. They must act in response to the rhythms of their age. Their genius must be adapted, in a phrase of William James's, "to the receptivities of the moment." Leaders are useless without followers. "There goes the mob," said the French politician hearing a clamor in the streets. "I am their leader. I must follow them." Great leaders turn the inchoate emotions of the mob to purposes of their own. They seize on the opportunities of their time, the hopes, fears, frustrations, crises, potentialities. They succeed when events have prepared the way for them, when the community is awaiting to be aroused, when they can provide the clarifying and organizing ideas. Leadership ignites the circuit between the individual and the mass and thereby alters history.

It may alter history for better or for worse. Leaders have been responsible for the most extravagant follies and most monstrous crimes that have beset suffering humanity. They have also been vital in such gains as humanity has made in individual freedom, religious and racial tolerance, social justice and respect for human rights.

There is no sure way to tell in advance who is going to lead for good and who for evil. But a glance at the gallery of men and women in *World Leaders—Past and Present* suggests some useful tests.

One test is this: do leaders lead by force or by persuasion? By command or by consent? Through most of history leadership was exercised by the divine right of authority. The duty of followers was to defer and to obey. "Theirs not to reason why,/ Theirs but to do and die." On occasion, as with the so-called "enlightened despots" of the 18th century in Europe, absolutist leadership was animated by humane purposes. More often, absolutism nourished the passion for domination, land, gold and conquest and resulted in tyranny.

The great revolution of modern times has been the revolution of equality. The idea that all people should be equal in their legal condition has undermined the old structure of authority, hierarchy and deference. The revolution of equality has had two contrary effects on the nature of leadership. For equality, as Alexis de Tocqueville pointed out in his great study *Democracy in America*, might mean equality in servitude as well as equality in freedom.

"I know of only two methods of establishing equality in the political world," Tocqueville wrote. "Rights must be given to every citizen, or none at all to anyone . . . save one, who is the master of all." There was no middle ground "between the sovereignty of all and the absolute power of one man." In his astonishing prediction of 20th-century totalitarian dictatorship, Tocqueville explained how the revolution of equality could lead to the *"Führerprinzip"* and more terrible absolutism than the world had ever known.

But when rights are given to every citizen and the sovereignty of all is established, the problem of leadership takes a new form, becomes more exacting than ever before. It is easy to issue commands and enforce them by the rope and the stake, the concentration camp and the *gulag.* It is much harder to use argument and achievement to overcome opposition and win consent. The Founding Fathers of the United States understood the difficulty. They believed that history had given them the opportunity to decide, as Alexander Hamilton wrote in the first Federalist Paper, whether men are indeed capable of basing government on "reflection and choice, or whether they are forever destined to depend . . . on accident and force."

Government by reflection and choice called for a new style of leadership and a new quality of followership. It required leaders to be responsive to popular concerns, and it required followers to be active and informed participants in the process. Democracy does not eliminate emotion from politics; sometimes it fosters demagoguery; but it is confident that, as the greatest of democratic leaders put it, you cannot fool all of the people all of the time. It measures leadership by results and retires those who overreach or falter or fail.

It is true that in the long run despots are measured by results too. But they can postpone the day of judgment, sometimes indefinitely, and in the meantime they can do infinite harm. It is also true that democracy is no guarantee of virtue and intelligence in government, for the voice of the people is not necessarily the voice of God. But democracy, by assuring the right of opposition, offers built-in resistance to the evils inherent in absolutism. As the theologian Reinhold Niebuhr summed it up, "Man's capacity for justice makes democracy possible, but man's inclination to injustice makes democracy necessary."

A second test for leadership is the end for which power is sought. When leaders have as their goal the supremacy of a master race or the promotion of totalitarian revolution or the acquisition and exploitation of colonies or the protection of greed and privilege or the preservation of personal power, it is likely that their leadership will do little to advance the cause of humanity. When their goal is the abolition of slavery, the liberation of women, the enlargement of opportunity for the poor and powerless, the extension of equal rights to racial minorities, the defense of the freedoms of expression and opposition, it is likely that their leadership will increase the sum of human liberty and welfare.

Leaders have done great harm to the world. They have also conferred great benefits. You will find both sorts in this series. Even "good" leaders must be regarded with a certain wariness. Leaders are not demigods; they put on their trousers one leg after another just like ordinary mortals. No leader is infallible, and every leader needs to be reminded of this at regular intervals. Irreverence irritates leaders but is their salvation. Unquestioning submission corrupts leaders and demands followers. Making a cult of a leader is always a mistake. Fortunately hero worship generates its own antidote. "Every hero," said Emerson, "becomes a bore at last."

The signal benefit the great leaders confer is to embolden the rest of us to live according to our own best selves, to be active, insistent, and resolute in affirming our own sense of things. For great leaders attest to the reality of human freedom against the supposed inevitabilities of history. And they attest to the wisdom and power that may lie within the most unlikely of us, which is why Abraham Lincoln remains the supreme example of great leadership. A great leader, said Emerson, exhibits new possibilities to all humanity. "We feed on genius. . . . Great men exist that there may be greater men."

Great leaders, in short, justify themselves by emancipating and empowering their followers. So humanity struggles to master its destiny, remembering with Alexis de Tocqueville: "It is true that around every man a fatal circle is traced beyond which he cannot pass; but within the wide verge of that circle he is powerful and free; as it is with man, so with communities."

# 1

# The Eve of Self-Government

On Monday, September 17, 1956, Kwame Nkrumah was summoned to the palace of the British governor of the Gold Coast, Sir Charles Arden-Clarke. At the time, the Gold Coast was a British colony, valued for its rich mineral resources and agricultural products. For over a century, European nations such as Great Britain had established colonies in Africa, and they had influenced the economic and political life of the continent long before that. The Africans, however, were rejecting this system and were struggling for national independence.

For the past decade, Nkrumah had been leading his country's struggle to gain independence from Britain. After several years of increased unrest Britain had allowed elections in 1951. The results were decisive: Nkrumah's party controlled the Legislative Assembly. Nkrumah himself emerged as Ghana's most important political figure, both in and out of the assembly. In some respects, the assembly was similar to the House of Representatives or Senate in the United States. It had the power to debate issues of national importance and help determine the Gold Coast's economic and political policies.

> *A break in the established order is never the work of chance. It is the outcome of a man's resolve to take life to account.*
> —ANDRÉ MALRAUX
> French writer

**Prime Minister Kwame Nkrumah salutes celebrating citizens of the newly named country of Ghana on March 6, 1957, the first day of national independence after nearly a century of British colonial domination.**

Sir Charles Arden-Clarke, the colonial governor, pictured during a farewell tour in 1957, when the British formally withdrew from the Gold Coast. Arden-Clarke worked closely with Nkrumah to guide the Gold Coast toward self-government.

Britain, however, still controlled the state and its economy, and tensions between the British and Nkrumah's followers, who wanted complete independence from colonial rule, continued to build.

Nkrumah had been working closely with the British colonial governor, Arden-Clarke, ever since the 1951 election. Together, the two men attempted to solve the economic and political problems of the day and reduce tension between the British and the Africans. About a month before the governor had summoned him to the palace, Nkrumah had formally requested that the British grant his country full independence.

Nkrumah tells in his book *Ghana: The Autobiography of Kwame Nkrumah* how his doubts and fears evaporated when he arrived at the palace and saw the smile on Arden-Clarke's face. The governor shook Nkrumah's hand firmly and told him that he had just received a message from the British secretary of state for the colonies. Nkrumah quickly read through the document and learned that his country would be granted independence on March 6 of the following year. Arden-Clarke told Nkrumah, "This is a great day for you. It is the end of what you have struggled for."

Nkrumah answered that it was a great day for them both, as they had both worked to assure a peaceful and orderly transition to self-government for the people of the Gold Coast. Nkrumah then told Arden-Clarke that he wanted to deliver the news to the Legislative Assembly the next day.

As he left the Government House, Nkrumah trembled with joy. His country would soon become the first country south of Africa's Sahara Desert to be granted independence from colonial powers. At the

**Nkrumah's political thinking was greatly influenced by Jomo Kenyatta, a pan-Africanist with whom he worked in England. A leader of Kenya's self-rule movement, Kenyatta was jailed for nine years by the British authorities; he became Kenya's first president in 1964.**

time, nearly every sub-Saharan country was controlled by Great Britain, France, Portugal, or other European nations. The sole exceptions were Liberia, which had been established as a haven for freed American slaves in 1847, and Ethiopia, which had remained an independent kingdom for most of its history. Nkrumah was especially proud that his country had achieved independence with almost no violence or loss of life.

As he lay in bed that night, he recalled the past: he saw himself as a young schoolboy in a small town, as a successful scholar in the Gold Coast's largest city, as an impoverished student and political agitator in the United States and Great Britain. He remembered returning to the Gold Coast in 1947 and quickly becoming the most respected political leader in his country. He recalled the difficulties he faced while organizing the independence movement, the time he had spent in jail, and his eventual acceptance as a politician and leader.

As he lay sleepless, remembering the past, his thoughts also kept returning to a future day: "The 6th of March. *The 6th of March . . .,*" the date that independence would be granted.

The next day, on which he was to deliver the good news to his country, was also Nkrumah's 47th birthday. As he looked at himself in the mirror he wondered: "Is it possible that all men feel as young as I do on their 47th birthday?" When he went downstairs he greeted his mother, who noticed that he was in extraordinarily good spirits but did not question him. He had decided to save his surprise for her a little later, after he had made the public announcement.

At 10:45 A.M. he returned to the governor's house and was handed the dispatch from London that Arden-Clarke had shown him the day before. He decided to make the announcement to the Legislative Assembly at noon, the same time as the news would be broadcast in Great Britain.

The minutes passed slowly as Nkrumah awaited what he called the "most triumphant moment of my life." At noon, Nkrumah marched into the assembly and told the speaker that he had an announcement.

While Britain's economic and psychological domination of its colonies was often blatant, this Gold Coast postage stamp, featuring Britain's Queen Elizabeth II, suggests the subtler range of the colonial presence in everyday African life.

The noisy assembly soon became quiet, and Nkrumah proclaimed: "Mr. Speaker, with your permission, I should like to make a statement. With effect from midday today, the publication of two dispatches of vital importance to the future of our country has been authorized."

The assembly immediately broke into cheers. After they quieted down, Nkrumah continued. "They are the dispatch from the governor at the request of my government to the secretary of state asking him to declare a firm date for the attainment of independence by the Gold Coast, and the secretary of state's dispatch in reply."

Nkrumah went on to read the statement from the secretary of state announcing the March 6 independence date. He also noted that the British had agreed to allow them to rename their country

Ghana, after a medieval African kingdom where centuries before a high level of civilization had been attained.

The entire assembly was initially dumbfounded; then wild excitement broke out. Nkrumah was soon mobbed by supporters, who lifted him onto their shoulders and carried him into the streets, where throngs of people were assembling and singing an independence song: "There is victory for us."

Kwame Nkrumah had succeeded in leading his country to independence from British colonialism through nonviolent and democratic means. As the news spread, congratulations poured in from all over the world.

> *It was the revolution in the Gold Coast, ending in the state of Ghana, which had struck imperialism in Africa the blow from which it would never recover.*
>
> —C. L. R. JAMES
> West Indian writer
> and politician

**Mohandas K. Gandhi, pacifist leader of India's successful independence movement. Nkrumah's nonviolent "positive action" strategies closely mirrored Gandhi's doctrine that nonviolent "soul force" was a moral and effective means to achieve political and social progress.**

UPI/BETTMANN NEWSPHOTOS

18

Although the Gold Coast had won its struggle for independence, national liberation movements continued their struggle elsewhere in Africa. In Kenya, for example, Nkrumah's friend Jomo Kenyatta was organizing an independence movement, and its more militant wing, known as Mau Mau, was engaged in a bloody war with the English. In North Africa, the Algerian liberation movement was involved in an armed struggle with the French. Liberation movements in other parts of Africa were also rebelling against the especially repressive Portuguese colonial regime as well as against British, French, and Belgian rule. Many African countries, following Nkrumah's example, would achieve independence without armed struggle.

In 1956 Nkrumah gained worldwide recognition as a political leader who had won his country's independence. He went on to achieve international renown for his efforts to create unity among newly independent African nations. Indeed, until he was ousted by a military coup in 1966, there were few better-known or more respected African leaders.

Kwame Nkrumah was a complicated man who held several conflicting views during his lifetime. While he initially subscribed to the philosophy of nonviolent resistance developed by Mohandas K. Gandhi in his campaign for the independence of India, Nkrumah later came to advocate armed struggle and revolutionary war throughout Africa as the most effective means of liberation. Once his country had won its independence, he promoted a free market economy; a few years later he changed his policies and supported a socialist economy. Although his strategies changed, Nkrumah remained steadfast in his goal and vision: a united Africa, free from foreign domination.

THE BETTMANN ARCHIVE

**Beyond collective political gains, the struggle for freedom in African countries held profound emotional significance for many individuals. These soldiers in Algeria wept with relief and joy on learning of Algeria's independence in 1962, ending 132 years of French rule.**

# 2
# Early Life and Schooling

Nkrumah was born in the Gold Coast village of Nkroful sometime around September 21, 1909. His exact birthdate is unknown since records were not kept in the village where he was born.

Situated in an area known as West Africa, the Gold Coast's shoreline faced the Atlantic Ocean. Although the Gold Coast region was rich in gold, diamonds, bauxite, and other minerals, at the time of Nkrumah's birth the country was relatively undeveloped and there was little industry or manufacturing. Most of the 5 million people who lived there inhabited rural villages made up of simple mud huts. The villages were governed by councils of elders who elected a chief. The chief settled disputes, provided leadership, and received certain privileges. Traditionally, these chiefs sat on stools made of precious wood and often decorated with gold or silver. The stool was a symbol of the chief's power; when he lost his authority, the privilege of sitting on the stool would be taken away and given to a new chief.

The colony was called "Gold Coast" because the West Africans who lived there had sold European

*In these European possessions whites ruled and non-whites obeyed. All the European empires in Africa were empires of race, where there was little place for an educated African.*
— J. AFRICANUS HORTON
West African scientist
and writer

**Nkrumah's belief that black and white people could work together to end injustices was fostered by educational experiences in his homeland and in Depression-era America. This 1939 yearbook portrait shows him as a senior at Lincoln University, the first all-black men's college in the United States.**

A busy marketplace in the coastal city of Keta. Market trading in cities and villages was traditionally conducted by women, who provided a conduit for news and local issues and came to be relied on by independence politicians as valuable allies and effective publicists.

traders gold since its discovery by the Portuguese, who had established a trading post there in 1482. Though the name initially referred only to the region's 200-mile coastline, it eventually encompassed several interior provinces and an area of around 92,000 square miles — slightly bigger than the whole of Great Britain, which dominated the region by the mid-19th century. In 1874 the Gold Coast was given official status as a British colony, and a colonial government was set up. All the important government functions were controlled by British administrators or Africans carefully selected and trained by the British.

At the age of three, Nkrumah and his mother, with whom he was very close, went to live with his father, a goldsmith in a neighboring village. Nkrumah was an only child, but he had many stepbrothers and stepsisters: like many African men, Nkrumah's father had more than one wife and thus a large family. In his autobiography, Nkrumah writes: "Our playground was vast and varied, for we had the sea, the lagoon and the thrill of unexplored bush all within easy reach." Though he enjoyed the companionship that came with an extended household, Nkrumah wrote that he was happiest when he was alone, wandering off to spend hours quietly observing the birds and other animals of the countryside.

The young Nkrumah did well in his studies and

Chieftains of the Gold Coast's powerful Ashanti tribe retained ceremonial traditions and their own political strength despite colonization. Much natural wealth — in the form of gold, cocoa, bauxite, and timber — is concentrated in the Ashanti region.

became a student teacher at the local school at the age of 17. The principal of the Government Training College in Accra, the capital of the Gold Coast, visited the school where Nkrumah was teaching one day. The principal was so impressed that he recommended that Nkrumah attend the college to further develop his skills as a teacher, and Nkrumah enrolled in 1927.

Life in the big city of Accra was quite different from the peaceful village life that he had previously experienced. Still, he made the transition smoothly. Nkrumah threw himself into his studies and a wide range of student activities.

He quickly came under the influence of Dr. Kwegyir Aggrey, an inspiring teacher and an accomplished public speaker. Often addressing large crowds, Aggrey urged those who gathered to hear his speeches to acknowledge their vital African heritage and gain confidence in themselves and their fellow countrymen. Aggrey was the first to arouse Nkrumah's national and racial pride, and he also instilled in the young student a belief that black and white people could work together for the liberation of Africa from foreign rule. This belief was one that Nkrumah held throughout his life and was not shared by all black nationalists.

Nkrumah graduated from the Government Training College in 1930. For the next five years he taught at a number of schools in the Gold Coast. He also began to think about furthering his studies in the United States. He applied for admission to Lincoln University in Pennsylvania, a school for blacks. Nkrumah filled out the admission papers, gathered letters of recommendation, and then visited the neighboring country of Nigeria to borrow money from a wealthy relative, who gave him £100 (then worth around $300).

Shortly thereafter Nkrumah received an acceptance letter and admission card from Lincoln. He traveled to the United States by ship, stopping off in England, where he met members of the emerging African independence movement. The Italian dictator Benito Mussolini invaded Ethiopia while Nkrumah was in England. Overcome with anger,

*He had not only done well at his books and games; he had also shown a rare determination and self-discipline.*

—BASIL DAVIDSON
British historian, on
Nkrumah's school days

Nkrumah vowed to struggle against foreign domination of Africa. "My nationalism surged to the fore," he later wrote. "I was ready and willing to go through hell itself, if need be, in order to achieve my object."

Once in the United States, Nkrumah realized that his funds were short. He immediately went to the college dean and explained his financial difficulties. Nkrumah said that he was willing to work his way through school, and the dean agreed to let him enter the freshman class if he passed the entrance exam.

Lincoln University had been founded in 1854 and was the first institution in the United States devoted to the higher education of blacks. Nkrumah was an enthusiastic scholar and graduated in 1939 with a degree in economics and sociology. He was described as a "most interesting" student by his classmates and did especially well in debates.

Nkrumah had originally planned to pursue his studies at the Columbia University School of Journalism in New York but found he could not afford the tuition. Luckily, he was offered a job teaching

Nkrumah (standing, rear right) with other student instructors from Lincoln University. His experiences as a teacher and at political meetings helped develop Nkrumah's skill as an orator and organizer.

philosophy at Lincoln and was able to enroll at the Lincoln Theological Seminary later that year. During this period, Nkrumah diligently read all the great philosophers. He was especially interested in social philosophy, and his later political speeches were peppered with quotations from thinkers such as Plato, Karl Marx, and John Stuart Mill.

For the next few years, Nkrumah continued to excel as both a student and teacher. In 1942 Nkrumah received both a master's degree in education from the University of Pennsylvania and a bachelor's degree in theology from Lincoln. He received another master's degree, in philosophy, the following year. In 1945 he was voted the "most outstanding professor of the year" by the students at Lincoln University.

During his ten years in the United States, Nkrumah experienced difficulty finding enough work to survive. The country underwent a period of economic depression in the 1930s; millions were unemployed and jobs were scarce. To afford graduate study he took on part-time jobs, many involving difficult manual labor, such as a job at a shipbuilding yard (where he caught pneumonia). His exposure to poverty and suffering made Nkrumah sensitive to the problems of the poor.

Nkrumah also witnessed firsthand the unjust treatment of blacks in the United States. He was shocked to learn that he could not eat or drink in certain restaurants or use certain public restrooms since segregation laws separated blacks and whites in eating establishments, shops, and on public transportation in many regions of the country.

Nkrumah also spent much of his time preaching in black churches. He became friendly with many people in the black community and gained insight into the lives of black Americans and invaluable experience in the art of public speaking.

Throughout his life, Nkrumah firmly believed in Christian values. While a theology student at Lincoln he wrote to Dr. George Johnson, dean of the Lincoln Theological School: "The burden of my life is to live in such a way that I may become a living symbol of all that is best both in Christianity and in the laws, customs and beliefs of my people. I am a Christian and will ever remain so, but never a blind Christian." Later he frequently called himself a "nondenominational Christian," which suggests that while he did not subscribe to the views of any one particular church, he continued to believe in the values of Christianity.

Nkrumah was also active politically during his stay in the United States. He worked to set up an African studies section at the University of Pennsylvania and organized the African Students' Association of America and Canada. He was elected first president of this group, and he also helped

**Direct exposure to American racism and segregation shocked Nkrumah during the 10 years he spent in the United States. Blacks, like this man in Oklahoma City in 1939, were often made to use separate fountains, rest rooms, and other public facilities.**

launch a newspaper called *African Interpreter*, which attempted to inspire feelings of African nationalism among both black Americans and Africans.

Already debates were taking place on how Africa could best emancipate itself from foreign domination. One view held that African liberation should proceed locally, with each country working out its own independence separately from other countries, while another maintained that the liberation of Africa would best succeed with activists in various countries coordinating their efforts, a process that would culminate in the liberation and unification

**The 19th-century Italian patriot Giuseppe Mazzini fought to consolidate his country's different kingdoms into a single, strong republic. His writings were among those Nkrumah studied while developing his vision of an independent, unified Africa.**

of all of Africa to form the United States of Africa. Nkrumah's goal was West African unity, and he and others from the region pledged to work for the liberation of the entire region, not just their respective nations. Although this proved impractical, such thoughts remained with Nkrumah his whole life.

Nkrumah carefully studied the works of the black nationalist Marcus Garvey while he was in the United States. His ideas on African liberation were influenced by the book *Philosophy and Opinions of Marcus Garvey*, which was published in 1923. Garvey espoused a philosophy of "Africa for the Africans" and began the back-to-Africa movement, which influenced many black Americans.

Garvey was a separatist, believing that blacks must take responsibility for their own lives and governments and not rely on white society in any way. He attempted to convince blacks in the United States and elsewhere to return to Africa and establish a black nation there. Garvey's passionate denunciation of racism in the United States and the colonial oppression of blacks in Africa by foreign countries greatly influenced Nkrumah's thinking.

Nkrumah also studied theories of political organization developed by the German economist Karl Marx, the Italian patriot Giuseppe Mazzini, the Russian revolutionary Vladimir Lenin, and others. He concluded that "whatever the program for the solution of the colonial question might be, success would depend upon the organization adopted." Accordingly, during the next several years Nkrumah embarked upon a search for the type of political organization that would best succeed in liberating his country, his region, and eventually all of Africa.

*I was parched with thirst and I entered the refreshment room and asked the white American waiter if I could have a drink of water. He frowned and looked down on me as if I were something unclean. 'The place for you, my man, is the spittoon outside,' he declared as he dismissed me from his gaze. I was so shocked that I could not move.*
—KWAME NKRUMAH
recalling an encounter with American segregation

# 3

# Man of Ideas, Man of Action

In May 1945 Nkrumah left New York for London after having spent 10 years in the United States. During his departure, he saw the Statue of Liberty "with her arm raised as if in a personal farewell to me. . . . 'You have opened my eyes to the true meaning of liberty,' I thought. 'I shall never rest until I have carried your message to Africa.' "

Nkrumah had planned to finish his Ph.D. in philosophy at England's Oxford University with the distinguished British philosopher A. J. Ayer. Instead, he became completely immersed in political activities and never returned to his studies.

Nkrumah joined the West African Students' Union and eventually became its vice-president. About a month after landing in London, he helped organize the Fifth Pan-African Conference, which was to take place that year. With the West Indian activist George Padmore, he became joint secretary of the organizing committee and intensified his involvement in the pan-African movement.

The pan-Africanists wanted to free the entire continent from colonial domination by the European

> *In order to restore self-government, we must unite, and in order to unite, we must organize. We must organize as never before, for organization decides everything.*
> —KWAME NKRUMAH

**Nkrumah in 1952, five years after his return to the Gold Coast. Overwhelming voter support for Nkrumah and his new Convention People's party (CPP) had forced the British to release him from a jail sentence the previous year.**

George Padmore, left, West Indian-born African liberation leader. As organizers of the 1945 Fifth Pan-African Conference, Padmore and Nkrumah set a historic precedent: the movement was at last being led by experienced political activists and organizers rather than intellectuals.

UPI/BETTMANN NEWSPHOTOS

*Imperialism is the endeavor of the great controllers of industry to broaden the channel for the flow of their surplus wealth by seeking foreign markets and foreign investments to take off the goods and capital they cannot use at home.*

—J. A. HOBSON
English economist

nations that had brutalized and exploited Africa for hundreds of years. Beginning in the 15th century, slave traders from Europe had captured black Africans and sold them as slaves in other parts of the world. In the 19th century European countries began taking direct control of the resources, lands, and peoples of the various African countries, setting up colonial governments to maintain their power. By the 20th century, blacks had begun to work to end the foreign domination of Africa and return the continent to native rule.

The Fifth Pan-African Conference took place in London in October 1945 and was a tremendous success. Two hundred delegates attended, and numerous reports were given describing conditions in Africa. An important declaration was written by Nkrumah and the renowned black American thinker and writer W. E. B. Du Bois, the cofounder of the National Association for the Advancement of Colored People (NAACP), which was formed to improve the status of blacks in the United States. In their joint proclamation, Nkrumah and Du Bois condemned the economic exploitation of Africa by the European powers and asserted the determination of Africans to be free from colonial domination. In particular, they spoke of the need for a political system characterized by "one man, one vote." As the Africans constituted the overwhelming majority of the population on their continent, such a system would give them potential democratic control.

In his own declaration, Nkrumah wrote: "All colonies must be free from foreign imperialist control, whether political or economic. The people of the colonies must have the right to elect their own government, a government without restrictions from a foreign power. We say to the peoples of the colonies that they must strive for these ends by all means at their disposal."

In an essay entitled "Toward Colonial Freedom," which was written in London around 1945, Nkrumah maintained "an uncompromising opposition to all colonial policies." He began his article by stating, "The aim of all colonial governments in Africa

W. E. B. Du Bois, the influential American writer, scholar, and civil rights activist. A champion of African nationalism, he became a citizen of Ghana in 1961. He and Nkrumah issued a joint declaration at the Fifth Pan-African Conference emphasizing colonial peoples' determination to achieve autonomy.

**European colonial powers earned harsh criticism for exploiting colonies as markets for their surplus goods. These World War II-era billboards promoting British-made products to Africans show this practice at work.**

and elsewhere has been the struggle for raw materials; and not only this, but the colonies have become the dumping ground, and colonial peoples the false recipients, of manufactured goods of the industrialists and capitalists of Great Britain, France, Belgium and other colonial powers who turn to the dependent territories which feed their industrial plants. This is colonialism in a nutshell."

Nkrumah went on to define what he meant by a colonial empire: "This is the conception of empire: diverse peoples brought together by force under a common power. It goes back to the idea of Alexander the Great with his Graeco-Asiatic empire."

At the time Nkrumah was writing this, Great Britain was the greatest colonial power in the world, and his native country, the Gold Coast, was part of that sprawling empire. He believed that the emancipation of his people from economic exploitation required a struggle toward political independence: "The basis of colonial territorial dependence is economic, but the basis of the solution of the problem is political. Hence political independence is an indispensable step toward securing economic emancipation." Nkrumah concluded that the road to independence from colonialism centered on national liberation movements, which would organize Africans to fight for their freedom.

In accordance with these beliefs, Nkrumah and his friends in London formed a West African National Secretariat to work to establish self-government for all the countries currently under British and French control in that region. Nkrumah became the general secretary of this group and worked tirelessly to promote its cause. The group founded a newspaper called *The New African*, organized a West African conference in London, and formed a Coloured Workers' Association of Great Britain to improve the living and working conditions of blacks living in Great Britain and coordinate activities between African students and workers.

While Nkrumah agitated in England for the emancipation of West Africa, events taking place in his native Gold Coast would soon allow him to put his ideas into practice.

In 1947 a group of African lawyers, merchants, and professionals in the Gold Coast formed an organization called the United Gold Coast Convention (UGCC). This group called for a constitutional convention to establish a form of government that would allow the natives of the Gold Coast to rule themselves as a relatively independent country within the British Commonwealth, much like Canada. The UGCC's members realized that if they wished to succeed, they needed to recruit and organize a cross section of the population in order to represent the interests of the entire country.

Kwame Nkrumah seemed to be the man for this task — he was already known as a man with great abilities as a communicator and a strong commitment to African independence. The members of the UGCC invited Nkrumah to return home to serve as general secretary of their organization. After discussing their proposal with his friends in London, he set sail for Africa.

Nkrumah had been away from the Gold Coast for

nearly 13 years. When he had left, his country was relatively peaceful. However, around 1947 a "swollen-chute" disease began to disrupt the vital cocoa industry, causing great concern about the economy. Opposition to British rule began to emerge. In January 1948 a chief in Accra named Nii Kwabena Bonne III began a boycott on the purchase of goods imported from England.

Events came to a head when the Ex-Servicemen's Union planned a march to present their grievances to the British colonial government. Many of these former soldiers had fought for the British Empire in World War II and felt that Britain should grant the Gold Coast independence, just as it had granted India independence in 1947. The servicemen marched on the Christiansborg Castle, the residence of the British governor. A squad of police blocked their way and fired on the crowd. Two people were killed and several were wounded.

When news of the shooting reached the marketplace in Accra, there was a riot. Mobs broke into shops owned by Europeans and looted their mer-

Cocoa beans, the country's most important agricultural product, being set out to dry. An epidemic of cacao tree disease shook the Gold Coast economy in 1947; British indifference to the growers' plight fueled support for Nkrumah's independence movement.

UPI/BETTMANN NEWSPHOTOS

chandise. The disorder continued for two days. By the time order was restored, 15 people had been killed, many more were injured, and a considerable amount of property had been destroyed.

A prominent member of the UGCC, Dr. J. B. Danquah, cabled the British colonial secretary, claiming that civil authority had broken down and requesting authority to form a government that could restore order. Nkrumah sent telegrams to several foreign governments and press agencies informing them of the unrest within the country. The British denied Danquah's request for a new interim government, but established a commission of inquiry to look into the causes of the recent disturbances.

Although Nkrumah had just returned to the country when the unrest broke out and had not actually participated in the recent demonstrations, he was arrested along with other top leaders of the UGCC. After two months he was released and began working in earnest to organize the people of the Gold Coast for independence.

**In 1948 African war veterans were shot at by white policemen while peacefully demonstrating at Christiansborg Castle, the governor's residence pictured here.**

# 4
# The Struggle for Independence

In 1948 Nkrumah traveled from one end of the country to the other to encourage people to join the UGCC. He explained in simple terms how the people of the Gold Coast were being exploited by the British. He lectured on national history and explained the independence program of the UGCC, patiently describing what was meant by universal suffrage, an elected assembly, and a parliamentary system in which each individual could vote for representatives who would govern in the people's name. Nkrumah also called for national unity and the end of tribal divisions.

During the next two years, Nkrumah traveled throughout the Gold Coast in a battered old car that often broke down. He frequently slept beside the road or in the huts of the villagers. The fervor of his campaign and his reputation as a spellbinding orator attracted people from miles around.

By 1950 the UGCC claimed a membership of between 1 and 1.5 million people out of a total population of less than 5 million. In addition to his traveling and political organizing, Nkrumah estab-

*There is no surer way to learn the art of revolution than to practice it.*
—KWAME NKRUMAH

**Nkrumah campaigned skillfully and tirelessly for the United Gold Coast Convention's (UGCC) independence drive. His dedication and skill as an orator quickly made him the preeminent figure in the Gold Coast's struggle for self-government.**

lished a system of colleges and schools to educate the largely illiterate citizenry and founded several newspapers to advance the goal of national independence. As he described it, "Day by day in [his newspapers'] pages the people were reminded of their struggle for freedom, of the decaying colonial system and of the grim horrors of imperialism." The motto of his most successful newspaper, the *Accra Evening News*, was "We prefer self-government with danger to servitude in tranquility."

Nkrumah was by now the most influential political figure in the Gold Coast's independence movement, but he found himself constantly at odds with the more conservative members of the UGCC. They were worried by his growing influence and increasing impatience with the British authorities. Matters came to a head when Nkrumah organized a nation-

As Nkrumah's personal popularity soared, his charisma and righteousness of purpose were often identified with those of Jesus Christ and spawned a cult known as Nkrumahism. Postcards like this one were sold in markets throughout Ghana.

WELL DONE THOU GOOD AND FAITHFUL SERVANT

SEEK YE FIRST THE POLITICAL KINGDOM AND THE REST WILL BE ADDED UNTO YOU

Dr Kwame Nkrumah, Prime Minister

UPI/BETTMANN NEWSPHOTOS

40

alist youth movement. At the time, the motto of the UGCC was "Self-government in the shortest possible time," while Nkrumah's youth movement adopted the motto, "Self-government now!"

Eventually the more conservative UGCC members asked Nkrumah to either disband the youth group or resign from the party secretariat. The youth organization was holding a conference at this time and called for the formation of a political party that would be independent of the UGCC. Nkrumah was hesitant to split the independence movement, so he met with the other members of the UGCC and finally decided to give in to that group's demands: he would return to his post as general secretary of the UGCC and disband the youth group. Word of his decision reached the expectant crowds that had gathered outside the meeting hall, and they managed to get a message to Nkrumah telling him to step outside. He did, and was greeted with cries of "Resign and lead us and we shall complete the struggle together!"

On June 12, 1949, Nkrumah announced the formation of the Convention People's party (CPP) before an audience of about 60,000 people. He explained why he thought that the time was right for "self-government now" and why a political party was the most effective vehicle to reach this goal. "The time has arrived," he declared, "when a definite line of action must be taken if we are going to save our country from continued imperialist exploitation and oppression."

Nkrumah's speech was received with tumultuous applause, and he became the leader of the new party. He resigned from the UGCC, and the CPP quickly became the most dynamic and powerful political force in the country, one that became increasingly identified with Nkrumah's policies and ideas.

Meanwhile, throughout 1949 the British government had been working on a new constitution for the Gold Coast, one that would allow more African participation in government affairs. Nkrumah denounced the British proposals as inadequate. Instead, he demanded immediate self-government within the British Commonwealth, an association of independent countries that recognized the Brit-

*Nkrumah's party was not built one by one. It was a crusade, a revivalist campaign, and the villagers joined by the thousands.*
—C. L. R. JAMES
West Indian writer
and politician

**The greatest leader of the American civil rights movement of the 1950s and 1960s, Dr. Martin Luther King, Jr., speaking at the 1963 March on Washington. Like Nkrumah, King pursued a Gandhi-inspired course of civil disobedience and nonviolent resistance to win civil rights for blacks.**

ish monarch as the symbol of their free association.

Nkrumah proposed a strategy he called "positive action," which he later defined as "the adoption of all legitimate and constitutional means by which we could attack the forces of imperialism in the country. The weapons were legitimate political agitation, newspaper and educational campaigns and, as a last resort, the constitutional application of strikes, boycotts and non-cooperation based on the principle of absolute non-violence, as used by Gandhi in India."

In India, Mohandas K. Gandhi had used what he called "peaceful resistance" to organize his people against British control of India and had succeeded in leading his people to national independence. Nkrumah applied similar nonviolent direct action tactics in the Gold Coast — a strategy also used later by Dr. Martin Luther King, Jr., to win civil rights for blacks in the United States.

Nkrumah traveled throughout the Gold Coast to begin "positive action" campaigns and used his newspapers to publicize the cause. On December 15 Nkrumah proclaimed at a large rally in Accra, "Get ready, people of the Gold Coast, the era of positive action draws nigh." Meanwhile, the Trades Union Congress, which oversaw the union activities of over 30,000 workers, was preparing a general strike and people in the cities were preparing for a boycott of European stores and products.

The unions began a strike on January 6, 1950, and after two days of negotiations Nkrumah announced his support. The strike was successful; most African-owned businesses shut down and many thousands of people refused to work. The

*How is it possible, I asked myself, for a revolution to succeed without arms and ammunition? After months of studying Gandhi's policy and watching the effect it had, I began to see that, when backed by a strong political organization, it could be the solution to the colonial problem.*
—KWAME NKRUMAH

AP/WIDE WORLD PHOTOS

Nkrumah at one of the many press conferences he held to draw international attention to the Gold Coast's liberation movement. His message to the world was clear: "What we want is the right to govern ourselves, or even to misgovern ourselves."

**Without deep-water harbors, coastal cities like Accra were dependent on laborers and small boats to carry all import and export goods to and from shore. Modernization and economic development were top priorities in Nkrumah's plans for his government.**

strike encompassed all businesses and public offices except those engaged in maintaining essential services, such as hospitals. Stores were closed, the trains and public transportation ground to a halt, and government services ceased.

Although people soon returned to work, Nkrumah believed that this first example of "positive action" was by and large a success. He later reflected: "The people had seen with their own eyes the economic life of the Gold Coast brought to a halt by unified people's efforts in the form of a general strike. Never again would they accept that it was hopeless to attempt to attack a seemingly mighty power structure as that represented by the colonial administration. The 'paper tiger' had been exposed, and this was the essential first step in its destruction."

The British government saw that they had a serious problem on their hands and quickly arrested Nkrumah and some of the leaders of his party. Nkrumah was sentenced to three years in jail. During his incarceration, he and his colleagues suffered greatly from poor nutrition, unsanitary conditions, and overcrowding in the cells, but Nkrumah kept his spirits up and communicated with the party by

UPI/BETTMANN NEWSPHOTOS

writing messages on toilet paper and having them smuggled to his associates on the outside. Moreover, Nkrumah's popularity had never been greater; he was more clearly than ever identified with his people's aspirations for self-government.

While Nkrumah was in prison his party continued to organize and agitate for independence. Although assertive political action was impossible because the British were ready to violently suppress any organized political force, Nkrumah's supporters marched and sang songs of independence in the streets. Newspapers published articles praising Nkrumah's courage and his party's dedication.

Meanwhile, the British government prepared for an election. Colonial law stipulated that anyone sentenced to more than a year in jail was ineligible to vote. Although Nkrumah was sentenced to three years in jail, the British authorities were forced to allow him to vote because he was serving three consecutive one-year terms. As a voter, he was also entitled to run for office, so the CPP was able to place his name on the ballot to run for the parliamentary seat from Accra. Nkrumah's candidacy, based on the clever exploitation of a legal technicality, received an enormous amount of support: he received 22,780 votes out of a possible 23,122, and the CPP won 34 out of a possible 38 seats.

Support for Nkrumah and the CPP was obviously much stronger than the British had imagined. Fearing widespread and possibly violent mass unrest, the British decided to release Nkrumah and allow him to form and lead a government.

Thus on the morning of February 12, 1951, Nkrumah was released from prison and assumed the title of leader of government business. In an address to the CPP members who had been elected to the assembly, he stated: "The die is cast, the exploited and oppressed people of colonial Africa and elsewhere are looking up to us for hope and inspiration. Progressive people in Britain and elsewhere are also solidly behind us. The torch of the Liberation Movement has been lifted up in Ghana for the whole of West Africa, and it will blaze a trail of freedom for other oppressed territories."

AP/WIDE WORLD PHOTOS

**As the Gold Coast's leader of government business, Nkrumah inspired exploited and oppressed people throughout colonial Africa and the world. As independence drew near for the Gold Coast he declared, "The die is cast."**

# 5

# "Hour of Triumph"

Almost immediately upon becoming the top African official in the new government, Nkrumah was awarded a doctor of law degree by Lincoln University. He made a triumphant return to his alma mater in the United States in 1951. In addition to receiving the honorary degree, he was able to see many old friends, and he received the key to the city of Philadelphia.

In interviews with the American media, he told of the Gold Coast's struggle for independence: "What we want is the right to govern ourselves, or even to misgovern ourselves." He spoke of the need for technicians, teachers, machinery, and economic aid to develop the Gold Coast and invited black Americans to live and work in his country to help his people develop a more modern society. Nkrumah was also received at the United Nations and spoke with U.S. State Department officials about aid for his country. On his way home, he reiterated his desire for complete national independence in a meeting with representatives of the British government.

Nkrumah was now an important leader known throughout the world. By 1952 his title was changed

*There's always something new out of Africa.*
—PLINY THE ELDER
1st-century Roman scholar

**Nkrumah triumphantly enters the first all-African parliamentary session of a free Ghana in 1957. His adoption of traditional native clothing helped to renew his nation's long-suppressed pride in African heritage.**

AP/WIDE WORLD PHOTOS

**47**

**Nkrumah (second from left) meets with UN officials during his 1951 trip to the United States. Also shown is Dr. Ralph Bunche (far left), the American scholar and diplomat who was the first black to be awarded the Nobel Peace Prize.**

to prime minister, giving him increased political power and prestige. But despite his enlarged role in the Gold Coast's government, Nkrumah and his African compatriots still did not control political affairs. The British governor still had tremendous authority and appointed many of the key ministers in the areas of defense, foreign affairs, finance, and justice. In addition, the civil service bureaucracy, which administered government programs, was dominated by the British, or by British-trained Africans who were primarily loyal to the British Empire. More than ever before, Nkrumah saw that if his country were to control its own affairs, it would be necessary to end British rule.

Nkrumah worked tirelessly for this objective. In 1953 he made his famous "motion of destiny" speech, which called upon Britain to make constitutional and administrative arrangements for independence. He asserted that "there comes a time in the history of all colonial peoples when they must, because of their will to throw off the hampering shackles of colonialism, boldly assert their God-given right to be free of a foreign ruler."

Nkrumah called for immediate constitutional reform and an act of independence that would specify a date and process for the attainment of complete self-government. He began to work with the British governor, Sir Charles Arden-Clarke, to attain his goal.

**Acclaimed American jazz trumpeter Louis Armstrong (left) and his wife made a point of stopping in the Gold Coast during a 1956 tour of Africa and Europe. Raised in the segregated South, Armstrong used his fame to further black causes.**

**Ballot boxes are transported to a counting station during the 1954 elections. The ballot boxes were marked by symbols representing political parties — a red rooster, visible here, stood for Nkrumah's CPP — to assure fair voting privileges to those who could not read.**

During the 1954 election Nkrumah's opponents within the Gold Coast did their best to organize against him, but once again his party won a strong working majority. Nkrumah and the CPP were able to continue the work they had begun.

In 1954 Nkrumah sponsored the Cocoa Duty and Development Funds Bill, which was passed by the Legislative Assembly. The new law guaranteed that a fixed price would be paid to cocoa farmers and that funds from cocoa sales would be available for economic development. A fair price paid to cocoa farmers secured internal stability, while the govern-

THE BETTMANN ARCHIVE

ment relied on profits from the export of surplus cocoa to help finance its programs.

Cocoa farmers in the interior Ashanti region, however, resented the bill. They felt they were not getting a fair share of the cocoa revenues, since the world market price of cocoa was rising above the fixed price set by the new legislation. They also felt that the central government was not spending enough funds to develop their part of the country.

Nkrumah responded to these protests by pointing out that a large hospital facility, a new library, a national bank building, and new roads had been built throughout the Ashanti. Still, many in the region remained disgruntled. Nkrumah also received opposition from residents of the northern provinces

**The Ashanti province's gold fields. Nkrumah sought to redirect the profits from Ghana's natural resources — which had formerly been siphoned off by colonial powers — back into the country to foster economic and social development.**

The main street of Accra, festooned with banners for March 6, 1957, the day the Gold Coast won its independence from Great Britain and officially became the sovereign nation of Ghana.

and the Togoland region, who wanted more local authority. Nkrumah's opponents united around the demand for a federal government, one that would provide more local autonomy. Nonetheless, Nkrumah stood firm in his argument that only a strong central government, with regional governments subordinate to it, would allow for full economic and political development. The importance of this issue increased as the movement toward national independence accelerated. Nkrumah continued to campaign for self-government while his opponents focused on the issue of the shape the government would take once independence was achieved.

In May of 1956 Nkrumah successfully pushed a resolution calling for the creation of a constitution for the "sovereign and independent state of Ghana" through the Legislative Assembly. Nkrumah wanted the Gold Coast to be renamed after a former African kingdom that had established an impressive civilization centuries ago. Stories had long circulated about ancient Ghana's wealth, culture, and high level of civilization. For Nkrumah and others, the name "Ghana" symbolized the ability of Africans to develop their own advanced civilization, without the influence of other cultures.

The British, seeing that the independence movement had gained considerable momentum, agreed to Nkrumah's demands. They called for another election to determine whether the people preferred Nkrumah's proposals for a strong central state or his opponents' demand for a form of government that would grant more power to local authorities.

Prime Minister Nkrumah, center, first row, with the members of independent Ghana's first cabinet. "Ghana" had once been the name of a flourishing ancient African civilization of great sophistication and cultural achievement.

UPI/BETTMANN NEWSPHOTOS

**Hoisted on the shoulders of fellow Ghanaian officials, Nkrumah participates in a 1957 independence celebration. With Ghana's freedom secure, Nkrumah intensified his efforts on behalf of independence movements elsewhere in Africa.**

The election campaign was bitter and tense, but once again Nkrumah and the CPP triumphed. The party won 71 out of 104 seats, giving them a strong majority in the Legislative Assembly. They won all the seats in several regions and a respectable number of seats in every district, enabling the party to legitimately claim to represent the will of the entire country.

Nkrumah reached what he called his "hour of triumph," on September 17, 1956, when the British governor informed him that the Gold Coast would be granted independence on March 6, 1957. The next day he spread the good news to his countrymen, and his tremendous feeling of accomplishment was heightened by the jubilant response of the country to the news.

Nkrumah did not rest with the liberation of his

own country, however. In his autobiography, he describes how, "As I drove home, physically and mentally tired but indescribably happy and content, I reflected on the long and difficult road on which we had travelled towards the goal of independence. African nationalism was not confined to the Gold Coast — the new Ghana. From now on it must be pan-African nationalism, and the ideology of African political consciousness and African political emancipation must spread throughout the whole continent, into every nook and corner of it."

Accordingly, once power was achieved, Nkrumah began what he called "the fight on two fronts." In Ghana, the society and economy would be reconstructed so that the people themselves would control and benefit from their resources and labor; at the same time, Ghana would become actively engaged in the struggle for the total liberation and unification of Africa. "This is not an easy task," he wrote. "Many splendid armies in history have been known to go to pieces for trying to fight on two fronts at once. The Convention People's party, however, is a different type of army. It is the people's own political army, built by their sweat and labor and steeled through its battles with imperialism and colonialism so that this double fight can hold no terrors for us. We are determined to conquer and we shall conquer on both fronts."

*What right has any colonial power to expect Africans to become Europeans or to have 100 percent literacy before it considers them 'ripe' for self-government? Wasn't the African who is now considered 'unprepared' to govern himself governing himself before the advent of Europeans?*
—KWAME NKRUMAH

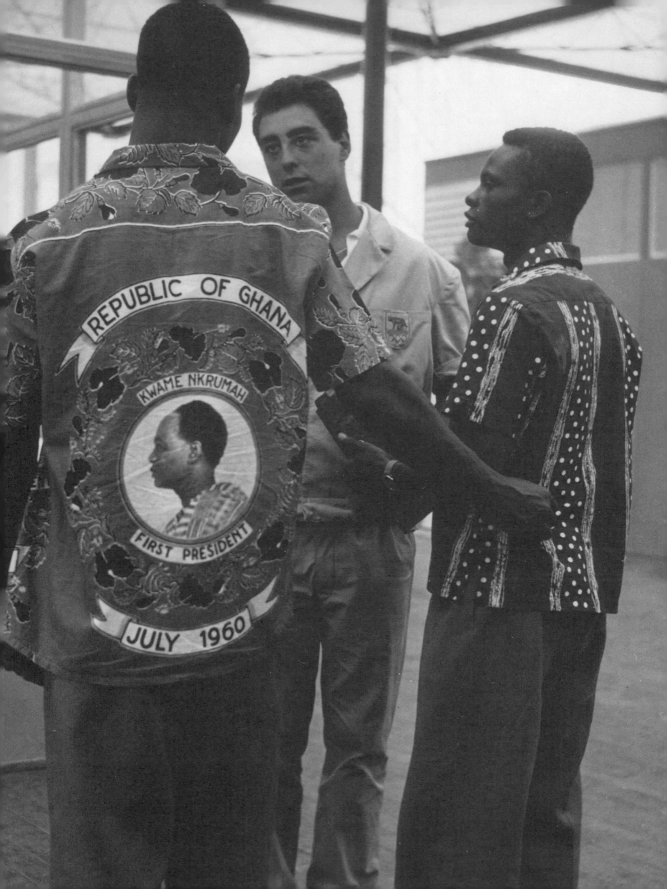

# 6

# The African Independence Movement

Almost immediately after obtaining independence, Nkrumah began working to consolidate ties with other independent African nations and to help more African countries win the right to govern themselves. Ghana hosted the Independent African States Conference in April 1958, the first attempt to organize those African countries that had already obtained independence. The All-African People's Conference, held in Accra in December of that year, was attended by representatives from trade union, cooperative, liberation, and youth movements from all over Africa. Nkrumah outlined his strategy for African revolution at the conference. He wanted to establish a pan-African organization that would "work actively for a final assault on colonialism and imperialism" and would "co-ordinate the efforts of all nationalist movements in Africa for the achievement of freedom." Later on in his speech, Nkrumah revealed that a major shift had taken place in his

*We are going to see that we create our own African personality and identity. We again re-dedicate ourselves to the struggle to emancipate other countries in Africa, for our independence is meaningless unless it is linked up with the total liberation of the African continent.*
—KWAME NKRUMAH
proclaiming
Ghana's independence,
March 6, 1957

The shirt worn by this member of Ghana's 1960 Olympic boxing team broadcasts his national pride and support for President Nkrumah. Eighty-seven countries participated in the Olympics in Rome that year; many were still under colonial rule.

**Nkrumah arrives at the UN in 1958. His goal that year was the creation of a pan-African group to coordinate all of the African independence movements.**

approach to revolutionary strategy. One of his proposals stated that Africans should "use non-violent means to achieve political freedom, but [should] be prepared to resist violence if the colonial powers resorted to force."

Representatives of the Algerian liberation movement, the National Liberation Front (FLN), were present at the conference. The FLN was embroiled in an armed struggle to free the North African colony of Algeria from French rule. Though Nkrumah himself had advocated only nonviolent methods to achieve independence, he was sympathetic with the plight of the Algerian people. He approved conference resolutions that justified the use of all means of resistance, including armed struggle, in the name of Algerian independence. As Nkrumah saw increased colonial oppression and violence being used against Africans, he would become even more sympathetic to the concept of armed resistance.

Another proposal called for delegates to "condemn racialism and tribalism wherever they exist and work for their eradication, and in particular to con-

demn the apartheid policy of the South African government." Nkrumah had assumed a leading role in the struggle against apartheid in South Africa and against the oppression of blacks in "settler regimes" such as South Africa and Rhodesia (which was renamed Zimbabwe after gaining independence in 1980). These regimes, controlled more by the whites who settled there than by Britain or any European power, tended to be even more racist and oppressive toward black Africans than European colonial governments.

Under South Africa's apartheid system, blacks had no political power or rights whatsoever and were forced to live in abject poverty in a totally segregated society. Nkrumah abhorred apartheid and did whatever he could to fight this oppression. In 1960 he passed a law that required any South African citizen entering Ghana to sign a document denouncing apartheid before being admitted, and he was partly responsible for South Africa's 1961 withdrawal from the British Commonwealth due to opposition to its apartheid policy.

Nkrumah was concerned with the political future of the entire continent, not just South Africa. He believed that political freedom was only the first step in the path toward independence, which also involved social and economic freedoms. In Nkrumah's view, true African independence required the full liberation and unification of the continent, because only if each African nation was able to control its own resources and to trade and exchange resources freely with other African countries could Africa hope to develop economically and meet the needs of its people.

Nkrumah undertook many practical steps toward his goal of African unification. In 1958 he formed a political union with the newly independent state of Guinea, an association that was intended to be a pilot scheme for a wider Union of African States. (The state of Mali joined the Ghana-Guinea union three years later.) Nkrumah also signed a secret agreement with Patrice Lumumba, the prime minister of the Congo, calling for a Ghana-Congo union. Lumumba, however, was assassinated before this

UPI/BETTMANN NEWSPHOTOS

**South Africa's foreign minister holds up a photograph of Nkrumah while alleging that although Nkrumah was critical of South Africa's apartheid policy, black South Africans were actually better-off than Ghanaians.**

UPI/BETTMANN NEWSPHOTOS

As the civil rights movement gained momentum in the United States, Nkrumah drew a large crowd at a speech he gave in New York City's Harlem in 1960. The strongest link between Africa and North America, he asserted, was America's 20 million blacks.

union could occur, and the Congo was taken over by forces who wanted nothing to do with the increasingly radical and outspoken Nkrumah.

In 1960 Ghanaians voted to approve a new constitution that changed Nkrumah's title from prime minister to president and provided for "the surrender of Ghana's sovereignty, in whole or in part, if at any time Ghana joined a Union of African States." This was the first time in history that an independent nation had given a constitutional guarantee that it would surrender its sovereignty to another body. The new constitution was perhaps the most profound demonstration of Nkrumah's commitment to the ideal of African unity.

Although Nkrumah was convinced that the benefits of African unity would outweigh regional differences, not all Africans agreed. In the early 1960s, the African states were divided into the two categories regarding the issue of unity. The more radical countries, which shared Nkrumah's views, held a conference in Casablanca, Morocco, in January

1961. These states — which included Ghana, Guinea, Mali, Libya, Egypt, Morocco, and representatives of the Algerian FLN — came to be known as the Casablanca powers. More conservative states, which were skeptical of plans for African unity, met in the Liberian capital of Monrovia in 1961. This conference was sponsored by Nigeria, Cameroon, Liberia, and Togo, nations that became known as the Monrovia powers.

In a speech at the Casablanca conference, Nkrumah stated, "I can see no security for African states unless African leaders, like ourselves, have realized beyond all doubt that salvation for Africa lies in unity. . . . for in unity lies strength, and as I see it, African states must unite or sell themselves out to imperialist and colonialist exploiters for a mess of pottage, or disintegrate individually."

*[The African educated elite] was caught in an awkward contradiction. They wished to assert and show the value of Africa's peoples, cultures, civilizations of the past; and that was one thing. But they also looked to Europe for guides and good examples; and that was quite another.*
—BASIL DAVIDSON
British historian

UPI/BETTMANN NEWSPHOTOS

President Gamal Abdel Nasser of Egypt, left, with Nkrumah at the 1961 Casablanca Conference, at which several neutral African states, Egypt and Ghana among them, adopted a policy of mutual defense and pledged to withhold support from nations that did not act in the interest of African unity.

**61**

The decades of colonial domination had left many Africans with a sense of cultural inferiority. Nkrumah worked to restore African pride. The Casablanca powers' Cultural Committee set up an Institute of African Studies to "safeguard African values" and promote a wider knowledge of Africa's contribution to societies and cultures throughout the world. Nkrumah commissioned the influential black American writer W. E. B. Du Bois, who had moved to Ghana in 1961, to coordinate work on an African encyclopedia that would document Africa's contributions to world civilization. In 1962 Nkrumah convened the First Africanist Conference in order "to discuss how best to promote scholarship and research into Africa's history, culture, thought,

Nkrumah greets W. E. B. Du Bois at a "World Without Bombs" anti-nuclear meeting held in Accra in 1962. Nkrumah asked Du Bois to supervise the compilation of an *Encyclopedia Africana*, although the project was never completed due to Du Bois's failing health.

AP/WIDE WORLD PHOTOS

UPI/BETTMANN NEWSPHOTOS

and resources." Nkrumah himself collected documents and made notes for a history of Africa he planned to write, though he was never able to realize this dream.

Nkrumah was also vitally concerned with questions of world peace and shared in the growing concern over the proliferation of nuclear weapons. When France tested a nuclear bomb in the Sahara Desert in 1960, increased levels of radiation were later detected throughout the continent. Nkrumah took the lead in protesting the testing of nuclear weapons on African soil. He supported resolutions to make Africa a nuclear-free zone and sponsored a "World Without Bombs" antinuclear peace movement in Ghana. In 1961 the Soviet Union awarded him the Lenin Peace prize for his efforts in promoting international peace.

**Radioactive fallout from 1960 French testing of nuclear bombs in the Sahara sparked widespread concern and angry charges of "nuclear imperialism."**

**Fathia, Nkrumah's Egyptian-born wife, with their eldest son, George Gamal Gorkeh Nkrumah, named after Egyptian President Gamal Nasser. Nasser helped arrange Fathia and Nkrumah's marriage, which was intended to promote unity between black and Islamic Africans.**

Regional conferences continued to take place throughout Africa, and in May 1963 a single, unified group, the Organization of African Unity (OAU), was created during a conference in Addis Ababa, Ethiopia. The organization had 32 original members, and only South Africa and South West Africa, a country whose government was controlled by South Africa, were excluded. Earlier that year, Nkrumah had published *Africa Must Unite*, a copy of which was given to every delegate at the conference. Although Nkrumah was one of the founding fathers of the OAU, he was disappointed when the conference ended and the group had not undertaken any significant projects.

Although the OAU had failed to establish an all-Africa governing body or a joint military high command as he had hoped, Nkrumah nonetheless left the conference resolved to continue working for African unity within the OAU. In a speech to Ghana's National Assembly in June 1963, he stated: "We have proved at Addis Ababa that we are ready to build a united Africa. . . . Until Africa achieves its total independence and national unification, the Af-

**Kwame and Fathia Nkrumah at a state banquet in 1961. Although their marriage was a happy one, Nkrumah and his wife were often separated after his ouster in 1966.**

rican revolution will not have completed its destined task. When we talk of African unity, we are thinking of a political arrangement that will enable us *collectively* to provide solutions to our problems in Africa."

Nkrumah's passion for African unity even surfaced in his private life. Although he had long claimed that he had no time for marriage or a family because of the political demands made on him, he decided to marry in 1963. Nkrumah wrote Egypt's President Nasser and expressed his desire to marry an Egyptian woman to help promote unity between North Africans and black Africans. In reply, Nasser sent Nkrumah information on three Egyptian women who he believed might be suitable, and Nkrumah selected Fathia Helim Rizik. Arrangements were made, and on the day of her arrival in Ghana in 1963, Nkrumah and Fathia were married at Christiansborg Castle.

**Nkrumah addresses the first meeting of the Organization of African Unity (OAU), in 1963. After the meeting, Nkrumah was disappointed by the OAU's failure to agree on a concrete agenda for Africa's future.**

**65**

# 7

# Ghanaian Socialism

As soon as he became leader of government business in 1951, Nkrumah began pursuing policies meant to modernize the country — a limitation on the power of tribal chiefs, the redistribution of land in the countryside, and a reorganization of the political and judicial system intended to insure all citizens full equality. Nkrumah's government also undertook crash education programs to increase literacy, improved communication throughout the country to lessen regional isolation, and began programs aimed at raising women's social status. The new government also attacked tribal myths and superstition and attempted to secularize education and politics.

The country, however, was so underdeveloped economically that modernization required a heroic economic development program. Nkrumah wrote that in 1951 "there was no direct railway between Accra and Takoradi, in those days our main port. . . . There were few roads, and only a very rudimentary public transport system. For the most part, people walked from place to place. There were few hospitals, schools or clinics. Most of our villages

*Capitalism is too complicated a system for a newly independent nation, hence the need for a socialistic society.*
—KWAME NKRUMAH

Nkrumah exhorts his fellow representatives at a 1964 meeting of the OAU to unite to protect independent Africa's hard-won freedom and to work together to foster the continent's economic development.

UPI/BETTMANN NEWSPHOTOS

67

**Women at a CPP rally in 1960. Women were often enthusiastic supporters of Ghanaian socialism, since it appealed to the sense of unity and common social purpose instilled by family and tribal ties.**

lacked a piped water supply. . . . It was not until we had grasped political power that we were in a position to challenge this, and to develop our resources for the benefit of the Ghanaian people."

But Nkrumah soon learned that there were definite limits to what he could accomplish, since from 1951 to 1957 Britain still maintained political and economic control within the Gold Coast. In fact, even after the country was granted independence in 1957, British interests continued to influence the economy and courts.

In retrospect, it appears that Nkrumah pursued two different economic policies during his time in power. From 1951 to 1961 he pursued what Bob Fitch and Mary Oppenheimer call in their book *Ghana: End of an Illusion* a pro-Western and anticommunist economic policy. From 1961 to 1966 Nkrumah pursued an increasingly socialist economic policy. What are the differences between these policies, and what results and problems did they produce?

In 1951 Britain controlled the Gold Coast economy almost completely, and cocoa was the colony's only major export crop. There was almost no industry or manufacturing, and British economic institutions dominated banking, finance, and trade. The civil service bureaucracy in the government was either British or British-trained and was primarily sympathetic to Great Britain's economic and political interests.

**Billboards erected at the time of Queen Elizabeth II's controversial 1961 tour of Ghana indicate the degree to which Ghana was still tied to Britain. Though he was now portrayed as the equal of the British monarch, Nkrumah had not shaken off his nation's economic dependency on Britain.**

**Vocational training programs for both sexes furthered two of Nkrumah's goals: the increased industrialization of economy and the emancipation of women.**

Given this situation, it was impossible for Nkrumah to do anything but work within the framework of the existing economic system. Any direct threat to British economic goals would have inevitably led to arrests or a military confrontation, since Britain would no doubt have reacted strongly to a challenge to its economic interests. Nkrumah was well aware of this situation. As he wrote in his autobiography, "it did not escape my notice that where the administrative service was concerned, if a policy was laid down for the officials by the government with which they disagreed, means were adopted, by subterfuge or otherwise to wreck that policy."

Thus even if Nkrumah had proposed radical economic policies during his first years in power, the bureaucratic and administrative branches of the government that were still dominated by the British could have sabotaged any plans with which they did not agree. Consequently, Nkrumah was initially moderate in his economic policies and attempted to combine a planned economy with a "free enterprise" system that was dominated by British corporations.

In 1951 Nkrumah launched a Five Year Development Plan, followed by a Consolidation Plan (1957–1959), and a second Five Year Development Plan (1959–1964). These plans included building a network of roads — later considered to be among the most modern in Africa — houses, schools, colleges, hospitals, and clinics. State enterprises and corporations were set up to further national trade and industry.

During his first years in power, Nkrumah had been guided by a development strategy formulated by economist W. Arthur Lewis that depended on foreign capital to industrialize the country. According to this strategy, a nonindustrialized country such as Ghana does everything possible to attract foreign investment so that money from wealthy capitalist countries can be used to build factories and modernize industry. For a country such as Ghana to be attractive to outside investors, it has to maintain internal order, guarantee the security of private enterprise and investment, and avoid close ties to the Soviet Union or any other communist country. Investors were fearful of the confiscation of industries and their assets that followed communist revolutions. The wise Third World leader, whatever his political sympathies, did well to give an impression of political stability and avoided earning a reputation as an admirer of communism if he wished to attract foreign investment.

Nkrumah followed this plan until 1961, when he realized that Britain was still the only capitalist country making large investments in Ghana and that these investments were producing few benefits for the country. Nkrumah decided that Ghana would have to depend on its own programs and resources to develop its economy.

> *What other countries have taken 300 years or more to achieve, a once dependent territory must try to accomplish in a generation if it is to survive.*
> —KWAME NKRUMAH

Nkrumah also concluded that a socialist organization of Ghana's economy was the only possible way the nation could control its resources and economic life. This meant that the state, and not foreign corporations or local economic interests, should play the dominant role in determining the economy's direction. It also required that the state, and not individuals, own and control industry, resources, banking, and foreign commerce.

Although Nkrumah wanted to expand the role of the state and the public sector in the economy, he did not pursue an all-out program of nationalization, in which the state seizes all industries and completely controls the economy, as in the Soviet Union or Cuba. Instead, Nkrumah pursued a more moderate course and focused on creating a mixed economy consisting of state and private enterprise and programs containing a mixture of private and public ownership.

Private enterprise would be gradually replaced by state enterprise, according to Nkrumah. That is, the state would take over more and more businesses and financial institutions — which were mostly still British-owned and controlled — and turn them into enterprises owned and run by the Ghanaians. Agriculture, an important part of the Ghanaian economy, would also be affected; Nkrumah hoped to create cooperatives where farmers would share farm implements and do agricultural work together, sharing the produce and profits.

Nkrumah later claimed that "the strategy was for the public sector, which controlled key areas of the economy, gradually to overtake the private sector until eventually the private sector was entirely eliminated. During this phasing out period, joint projects involving state and private enterprise were embarked upon."

While Nkrumah did not want to alienate the Soviet Union or any other socialist government, he intended to develop a socialist society specifically adapted to Ghanaian conditions. "Our aims," he stated, "embrace the creation of a welfare state based on African socialist principles, adapted to suit Ghanaian conditions, in which all citizens, regardless of class, tribe, color or creed, shall have equal opportunities. . . . We aim to create in Ghana a socialist society in which each will give according to his ability and receive according to his needs."

Nkrumah realized that he needed to educate Ghanaians about socialism if his new policies were to gain widespread support. "Socialism cannot be built without socialists," Nkrumah said. He recognized that conditions were not ideal for a rapid transformation of the economy: "Ideological education was being given top priority, but had still not

**In 1960 Nkrumah met with four other leaders — (from left) Jawaharlal Nehru of India, Nasser of Egypt, Sukarno of Indonesia, and Josip Broz Tito of Yugoslavia — to examine ways of developing socialist societies without imitating Soviet or other totalitarian systems.**

**Workers demonstrate in Accra in 1960. Low pay and unemployment were among the stubborn economic issues facing Ghana after its independence.**

reached a satisfactory level. Bourgeois [middle-class] economic interests were too entrenched to be removed entirely, or overnight. Ghana inherited, at independence, almost total trade dependence on the West. Our economy was almost completely foreign or local capitalist owned. The colonial mentality permeated the professions, and particularly the army, police and civil service."

To promote his socialist ideals, Nkrumah developed several mass organizations that constituted five separate wings of the CPP: the Trades Union Congress, the United Ghana Farmers' Council, the

74

National Council of Ghana Women, the Ghana Young Pioneers, and the Cooperative Movement. These organizations represented the main constituencies of the party (workers, farmers, women, youth, and those engaged in running state-supported cooperative organizations, such as dairies) and were created to express the interests of each group. They also served as instruments for mass mobilization and the spread of political propaganda praising the new economic programs and socialism in general.

To further promote socialism, Nkrumah established the Ideological Institute at Winneba. The institute would train students, government workers, and others in the principles of socialism and also serve to propagate Nkrumah's views and writings. He also encouraged the youth wing of his party, the National African Socialist Students' Association, to establish socialist study groups all over Africa.

The construction of Nkrumah's ideal socialist state also involved attempts to root out corruption. In a "dawn broadcast" to his country on April 8, 1961, Nkrumah attacked party leaders who were benefiting economically from Ghana's economic development. He insisted that members of his government could not receive government contracts and favors for businesses they owned or in which they had an economic interest. Moreover, Nkrumah stipulated that no top official in his government should own more than two houses with a combined value of £20,000 Ghanaian, more than two automobiles, or any additional land valued higher than £500 Ghanaian.

In addition, Nkrumah established a commission of inquiry, which examined the assets of all the important leaders of the CPP and investigated charges of government corruption. The commission's report showed that some national leaders were in possession of property far in excess of what they could have acquired honestly. Other politicians possessed more property than Nkrumah deemed proper. Many officials were fired from their jobs or forced to give up property; those found guilty of corruption were fired and prosecuted.

**Nkrumah with the Chinese leader Mao Zedong in 1962. Though leery of patterning his country's socialism too closely after another's, Nkrumah did seek technical assistance from other socialist and communist governments.**

In the "dawn broadcast," Nkrumah called his new socialist development program an attempt to reform his party. It was, he said, "a call to action to revitalize the Convention People's party, to end self-seeking, to energize the efforts of the people toward socialism. . . . Some party members in Parliament pursue a course of conduct in direct contradiction of our party aims. They are tending, by virtue of their functions and positions, to become a separate social group aiming to become a new ruling class of self-seekers and careerists. This tendency is working to alienate the support of the masses."

Nkrumah wanted his government to serve the interests of the people directly and sought to avoid the development of a privileged, corrupt ruling class that would be the primary beneficiary of Ghanaian economic development. Cleaning up corruption and attempting to eliminate privilege, however, alienated him from powerful forces in his party.

Nkrumah ignored his critics and continued to construct a socialist state. He believed that socialism provided a better road to economic development than capitalism, because with socialism the people themselves, rather than entrenched private interests, would theoretically own and control the nation's resources and wealth. Socialism, he believed, would also promote the values of national service, sacrifice, and the common good. He believed that the capitalist emphasis on the individual would inevitably lead to corruption and the enrichment of some people at the expense of others.

Nkrumah formalized his socialist economic programs in March 1964 with the launching of a Seven Year Development Plan. "Our aim under this plan," Nkrumah announced, "is to build in Ghana a socialist state which accepts full responsibility for promoting the well-being of the masses. Our national wealth must be built up and used in such a way that economic power shall not be allowed to exploit the worker in town or village, but be used for the supreme welfare and happiness of our people." Nkrumah claimed that the plan attempted to secure for every citizen "at the earliest possible date, an adequate level of education and nutrition and a satisfactory standard of clothing, housing and leisure."

According to Nkrumah, the Seven Year Plan was the first integrated and comprehensive plan for Ghana's economic development, since it was based on a careful study of national resources, industries, and economic needs. The goal of the plan was to achieve economic independence through industrialization and modernization. Nkrumah was especially interested in expanding the country's ability to produce manufactured goods, since he believed that Ghana would achieve economic self-sufficiency only if the nation moved away from an economy based on the exportation of raw materials and towards an economy based on the manufacture of finished products.

There were three chief elements to Nkrumah's new economic strategy. First, large industries would

> *To the black man in all parts of the world Nkrumah gave a new pride.*
> —*Legon Observer*
> Ghanaian newspaper

The abundance of certain native crops spurred Nkrumah's plans for agricultural industries as part of his Seven Year Development Program.

be constructed near the source of their raw materials. For example, sugar refineries and cocoa-processing plants would be built close to where the sugarcane and cocoa were harvested. Second, the program called for the development of more industries that refined native resources, such as factories that produced chocolate bars from Ghanaian cocoa and sugar. Light industries and small manufacturing could be set up for the production of essential goods such as shoes, clothing, and furniture. Finally, in order to protect the nation's economic interests, foreign investment and ownership would be appraised and regulated according to its contribu-

tions to Ghana's own economic development. Nkrumah maintained that foreign investment had to be controlled "to safeguard our socialist policy and national independence."

To provide the necessary electrical power to make his industrialization scheme possible, Nkrumah proposed constructing a dam and electrical plant on one of Ghana's major rivers. The Volta River Project would not only fulfill the nation's power needs but would also produce enough extra power to sell to neighboring nations, fostering the development of nearby regions while providing Ghana with important revenue to further develop its industries.

Nkrumah's government was especially interested in building a plant for the processing of Ghana's large bauxite reserves. Previously, the mineral had been processed outside of the country. Nkrumah planned to use the Volta hydroelectric power to fuel the plant, which would smelt the bauxite into aluminum, a more valuable commodity on the world market. The giant hydroelectric plant would cost around $140 million, of which Ghana would pay 50 percent. The rest would be provided by foreign loans and development agencies, many of which were U.S.-based. As Nkrumah later explained, "It was considered, in the circumstances of the time, that the undertaking of joint projects with already operating capitalist concerns was better than the alternative of economic blockade by the West and the consequent lack of development until the assistance of socialist states could be procured and become operational."

KWAME NKRUMAH
FOUNDER OF THE NATION

# 8

# Ousted

Kwame Nkrumah tried to steer a middle course between East and West, communism and capitalism. He ultimately decided to construct a socialist economy in Ghana, but one that would allow capitalist private enterprise and that would embark on joint economic projects with the capitalist countries. Although he pursued increasingly socialist policies and maintained ties with the Soviet Union, he kept Ghana free from the control of other communist nations. In foreign affairs, Nkrumah associated Ghana with the nonaligned countries — which avoided close association with both the United States and the Soviet Union — rather than with the socialist bloc.

Still, his increasingly vehement socialist rhetoric angered the leaders of capitalist countries. His 1965 book *Neocolonialism: The Last Stage of Imperialism*, angered Western governments, especially the United States, which cancelled a large foreign aid package after the book was published. Nkrumah claimed that overt colonialism had been replaced by neocolonialism, or the use of political and economic means to control less-developed countries. In his book he singled out the United States as the center

*Nkrumah was terribly alone. He had to govern through a civil service or through party factions, playing off one against the other. Somewhere beyond this network of administrative intrigue stood the people of the country, watching with indifference a political game in which they had no part. When the coup came, they too would be absent from the scene.*
—BASIL DAVIDSON
British historian

**A larger-than-life statue of Nkrumah was installed outside the Parliament House in Accra during the early years of independence; an inscription proclaimed him "Founder of the Nation."**

of the world neocolonialist system. Nkrumah argued that "the less developed world will not become developed through the goodwill or generosity of the developed powers. It can only become developed through a struggle against the external forces which have a vested interest in keeping it underdeveloped. Of these forces, neocolonialism is, at this stage of history, the principal."

Defining neocolonialism, Nkrumah wrote, "The essence of neocolonialism is that the state which is subject to it is, in theory, independent and has all the outward trappings of international sovereignty. In reality its economic system and thus its political policy is directed from outside." Nkrumah claimed that neocolonialism began after World War II, when Western colonial powers concluded that they could gain greater profits from African and other Third World countries by granting independence to these developing nations, thereby saving themselves the expense of administrating colonial governments and providing social services.

Instead, the neocolonialists believed they could best extract their profits if their corporations controlled the former colony's resources, industries,

Nkrumah and Chinese Premier Zhou Enlai toast the good relationship between their nations in 1964, a time when Western capitalist countries were angered by Nkrumah's penetrating attacks on neocolonialism and his turn to socialism.

and markets. Nkrumah claimed that foreign corporations were rapidly gaining control of Africa's gold, diamonds, and other wealth.

Nkrumah maintained that some African states were already controlled by neocolonial powers and said that while it made economic sense to enter into partnerships with foreign corporations to pursue certain projects, African states must be very careful in dealing with these corporations to avoid exploitation. In defending his own deals with multinational corporations and U.S. financial institutions, Nkrumah wrote, "We did not allow them to operate in such a way as to exploit our people. They were to assist in the expansion of our economy in line with our general objectives, an agreed portion of their profits being allocated to promote the welfare and happiness of the Ghanaian people."

While Nkrumah's charges of neocolonialism alienated many abroad, his socialist policies were making enemies at home. Conservative and antisocialist groups became increasingly critical of his domestic policies and began planning a rebellion against him. By 1966 there had been several attempts on Nkrumah's life, mostly by the military and police.

An attempt on Nkrumah's life by a police constable prompted this 1964 cartoon in a CPP newspaper. *Osagyefo* was a title Nkrumah adopted, meaning savior, redeemer, and messiah; many critics found the title objectionable.

**Nkrumah visits a woman injured after a bomb exploded in a crowded stadium after he had left. Repeated assassination attempts stalked Ghana's increasingly controversial leader.**

*In fact, the African's way of life even today is more democratic than the much-vaunted 'democratic' manner of life and government of the West.*

—KWAME NKRUMAH

Nkrumah had for years been unpopular with both groups. In his early days as an agitator for independence, Nkrumah had been critical of the chief of police. During those years, the police kept Nkrumah under constant surveillance, and he was twice arrested and jailed. Even after independence, Nkrumah always mistrusted the police, whom he believed had assimilated British colonial values and practices and never fully supported his regime. Likewise, Nkrumah believed that the military was disloyal to his government. Almost all the officers had been trained in England, and Nkrumah felt that they too had assimilated English values and were hostile to his government.

Eventually, he hoped to remove those hostile to his regime from the police and military and replace them with individuals who supported his government. However, a high crime rate and Nkrumah's desire to maintain a strong military forced him to retain many individuals who did not support his ideas and policies.

Some of the police and military who joined the conspiracy against Nkrumah were acting to protect their own interests, as they understandably feared that Nkrumah would eventually replace them with a people's militia. Some military men were made uneasy by Nkrumah's "African Defense Bill," which pledged that Ghana's troops would be sent "wherever the peace and security of Africa is threatened." In particular, they worried that Nkrumah would send Ghanaian troops to Rhodesia to fight the racist settler government there.

Nkrumah's opponents acted on February 23, 1966, after Nkrumah and several of his top aides had left for China to present North Vietnamese leader Ho Chi Minh with a plan to end the Vietnamese war. Rebel army leaders told their troops that

**Nkrumah meets with India's Prime Minister Indira Gandhi on February 22, 1966, two days before a coup staged by disloyal army and police officers stripped him of power.**

Nkrumah intended to send them to Vietnam and Rhodesia, that he had deserted Ghana with millions of stolen dollars, and that the Russians would take over the country if the troops failed to act. The rebels were able to convince some military and police units to attack Nkrumah's chief government office, the Flagstaff House, which was protected by loyal troops and Nkrumah's Presidential Guard Unit. Fighting was fierce, but the rebels were able to take over communications and force Nkrumah's loyal supporters to surrender by threatening to blow up the government headquarters and kill Nkrumah's family.

By 6:00 A.M. the next day, the police, acting on the command of the rebels, had arrested most of Nkrumah's ministers and other political allies, and the rebels were able to broadcast reports stating that the army and police had taken over the government.

**The Parliament House statue meant to immortalize Nkrumah was ripped from its pedestal and broken by rebel forces during the 1966 coup.**

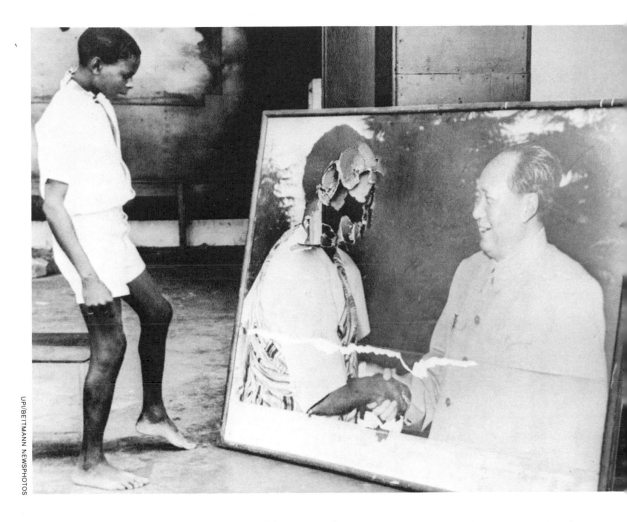

Although the U.S. ambassador to Ghana and some Western media described the military takeover as "bloodless," Nkrumah later claimed that probably more than 1,000 people were killed and many more wounded. In his book *Dark Days in Ghana* he contends that many atrocities were committed by rebel troops and also describes how they destroyed his house, government offices, manuscripts, and book collection.

Nkrumah claimed that "never before in the cherished history of our new Ghana had citizens, defenseless men and women, been assassinated in cold blood by their own soldiers. Not a single Ghanaian life was taken during the whole fifteen years

**A mutilated photograph of Nkrumah lies in the streets of Accra after the coup. The rebel government charged that Nkrumah's regime had been corrupt and had devastated the economy. Ghanaians did not rise to defend the man they had once idolized.**

> *It was indeed an inglorious ending for a man who once held such hope as a leader of global stature, a man whose gravest error may have been that in the final years he began believing he really was all the things he said he was.*
>
> —DAVID LAMB
> American journalist, on
> Nkrumah's overthrow

of my administration. There are few, if any, governments in the world which can say as much. Yet here was this handful of traitors at one blow spoiling our proud record, and dragging Ghana's name through the mud."

In recent years, allegations have been made linking the U.S. Central Intelligence Agency (CIA) with the plot against Nkrumah. Former CIA agent John Stockwell reports in his book *In Search of Enemies* that the CIA participated in the Ghana coup despite a congressional committee's rejection of a CIA plan to overthrow Nkrumah. Stockwell maintains that the CIA station in Accra "was nevertheless encouraged by headquarters to maintain contact with dissidents of the Ghanaian army for the purpose of gathering intelligence on their activities. It was

**Khow Amihyia, considered the engineer of Nkrumah's overthrow, was once described by Nkrumah as "my most dangerous enemy." Amihyia told reporters that he had received training from the U.S. Central Intelligence Agency (CIA).**

given a generous budget, and maintained intimate contact with the plotters as a coup was hatched. . . . The Accra station was given full, if unofficial credit for the eventual coup, in which eight Soviet advisors were killed. None of this was adequately reflected in the agency's written records."

In May 1978 a newpaper story appeared in *The New York Times* that gave further details of the CIA role in Nkrumah's overthrow. The author of the article, Seymour Hersh, concluded: "Many CIA operatives in Africa considered the agency's role in the overthrow of Mr. Nkrumah to have been pivotal."

The rebel government called itself the National Liberation Council and claimed that they were saving the country from Nkrumah's economic policies, which they maintained had bankrupted the country and destroyed the economy. They charged that Nkrumah and his government were hopelessly corrupt and had robbed the country of millions of dollars. They also promised to promote economic reform and return the country to civilian rule once law and order was restored. Despite the new regime's strong-arm tactics and charges of corruption against the head of the National Liberation Council, Lieutenant General Joseph Ankrah, the country did not rise to Nkrumah's defense.

**John Stockwell, former CIA agent. His book *In Search of Enemies* claims that well-financed CIA operatives stationed in Accra maintained close contact with rebel plotters.**

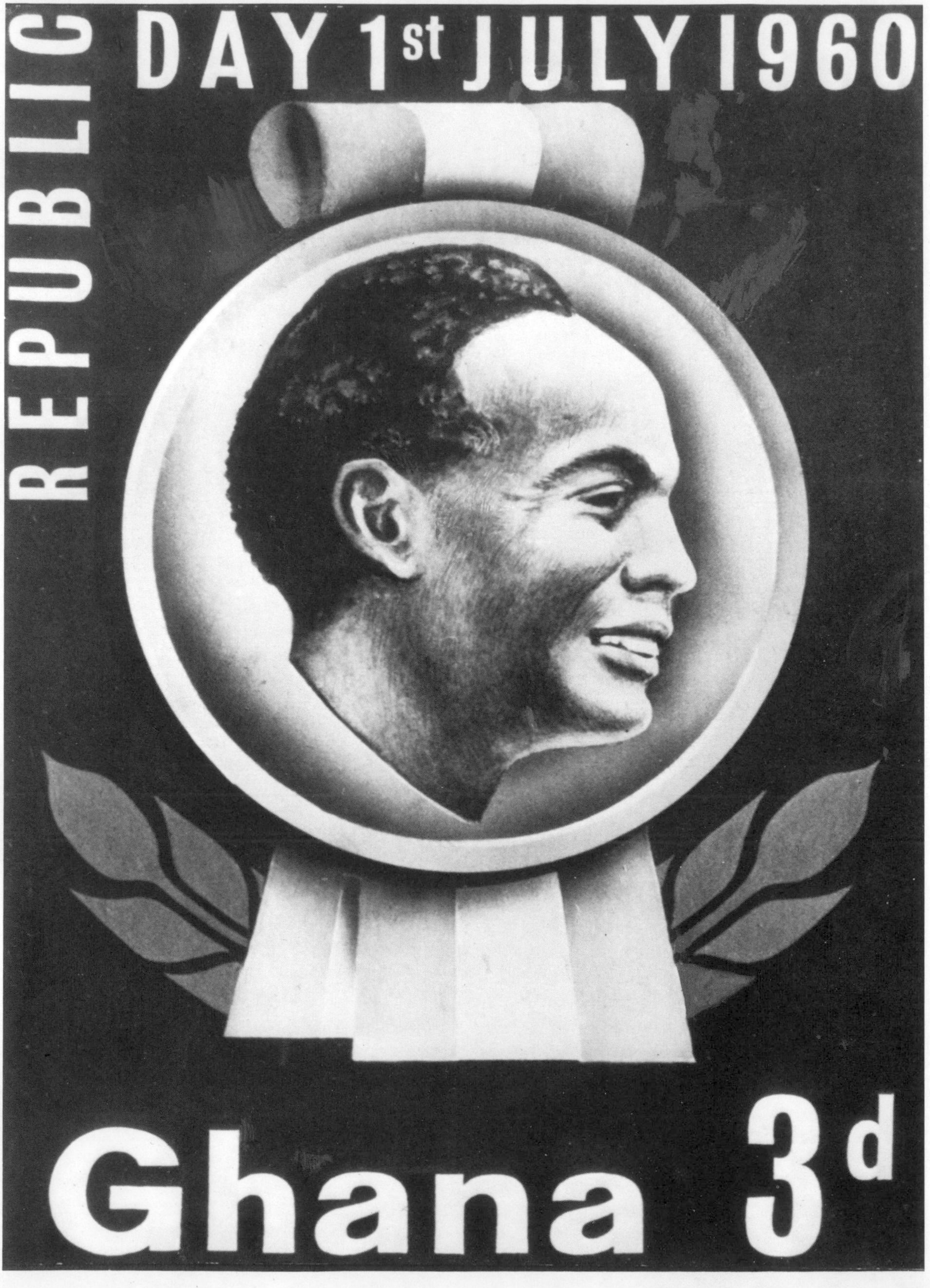
REPUBLIC
DAY 1st JULY 1960
Ghana 3d

# 9

# Nkrumah's Years in Power: Achievements and Mistakes

Once the most overwhelmingly popular figure in his country and the acknowledged leader of his country's struggle for liberation, Nkrumah had lost the support of significant segments of the people. One reason may have been that the populace resented the way in which Nkrumah handled power. He had taken on the name *Osagyefo* — which means savior, redeemer, and messiah — and had frequently abused his authority by jailing political opponents, firing judges who ruled against his wishes, and deporting journalists who criticized him. In 1964 Nkrumah pushed through a resolution, approved by his parliament and ratified by the people in a referendum, establishing a one-party state and declaring himself "party leader for life." Thus, in effect, Nkrumah demanded and received lifetime political control of his country.

In his defense, Nkrumah wrote, "A distinction must be made between the loss of freedom to subvert, and the loss of freedom of expression. At no

*For years, Ghana, through its extraordinary president, Nkrumah, was example, catalyst, inspiration, spearhead and pacemaker, passionate friend and infuriating irritant, to the rest of Africa.*
—MARION KAPLAN
British photojournalist

**A postage stamp issued in 1960, a time when Nkrumah enjoyed widespread support. Signs of alienation and resentment toward his methods surfaced later and grew when he declared himself "party leader for life."**

time has my government denied the rights of Ghanaians to hold political meetings and to discuss the country's affairs with complete frankness."

In his book *Ghana: Nkrumah's Legacy*, Kwesi Armah maintains that significant debate occurred within Nkrumah's government. Armah states that Nkrumah listened and often yielded to those who opposed some of his policies. He attempts to refute those who claimed that Nkrumah carried out a "ruthless dictatorship" and concluded that "within its rank and file the Convention People's party had men of courage who put their sense of public duty before all else; in its leader the party had a selfless patriot who put state interests above all personal considerations. This in fact was the basis of Nkrumah's power."

Many of Nkrumah's critics, within Ghana and around the world, however, contended that while Nkrumah may have begun as a "selfless patriot," he lost sight of the needs of his countrymen as he consolidated power and pursued his grand ideals of uniting all of Africa and creating a socialist state.

**Anti-Nkrumah sentiment ran high in the early days of the National Liberation Council (NLC); much of it echoed NLC propaganda. This demonstration took place less than two weeks after Nkrumah had been deposed.**

AP/WIDE WORLD PHOTOS

By the time of his overthrow, Nkrumah had managed to alienate vast sectors of his country. Earlier political struggles had left him at odds with certain conservative professional and political groups, and the firings that resulted from his campaign against corruption in his government created dissension in his own party. Many people were disappointed by his suppression of civil liberties and attempts to silence opponents. He also lost working-class support when he suppressed trade-union movements by only allowing government-controlled unions and disallowing strikes.

Perhaps the most serious charges leveled against Nkrumah were claims that he had ruined the national economy, while he and his ministers had enriched themselves at the country's expense. Former officials and associates testified that both Nkrumah

**Demonstrators protest the arrival of a representative from the NLC in London on September 6, 1966. Seven months after his overthrow, Nkrumah continued to receive support from many groups.**

**President Nkrumah in 1961, the year he became chancellor of the Kwame Nkrumah University of Science. His commitment to education brought concrete results: by the time of his overthrow, Ghana had one of the best educational systems of any independent African nation.**

and his associates took bribes, stole from the government, and had large foreign bank accounts.

Nkrumah mounted a vigorous defense against the charges that he was corrupt and had ruined the economy. In *Dark Days in Ghana* Nkrumah says that before he restructured the economy, "Ghana needed to be rescued from 'economic chaos' " and that the allegations against him served as "an umbrella excuse for the seizure of power by neocolonialist inspired traitors." Though he was accused of squandering Ghana's assets, Nkrumah claimed that the money he received when the Gold Coast was granted independence was invested in projects that served the needs of its people. He maintained that while his government had gone into debt, like most Third World countries, the debts were incurred to support projects that benefited all Ghanaians.

Nkrumah contended that it was the successes of

UPI/BETTMANN NEWSPHOTOS

his regime, not its failures, that led the army, police, and their allies to overthrow his government: "Ghana, on the threshold of economic independence, and in the vanguard of the African revolutionary struggle to achieve continental liberation and unity, was too dangerous an example to the rest of Africa to be allowed to continue under a socialist directed government."

Nkrumah argues in *Dark Days in Ghana* that the first development plans of his government from the 1950s up until the mid-1960s produced a skilled labor force and "an adequate complement of public services . . . such as transport, electricity, water and telecommunication." He detailed the primitive conditions in his country when he took office and concluded that "our first two Development Plans had been carried out with a high degree of success. We had one of the most modern networks of roads in Africa. Takoradi harbor had been extended, and the great artificial harbor at Tema, the largest in Africa, built from scratch. Large extensions to the supply of water, and to the telecommunication network had been constructed, and further extensions were under construction. Our agriculture was being diversified and mechanized. Above all, the Volta River Project, which was designed to provide the electrical power for our great social, agricultural and industrialization program, was almost completed."

Nkrumah maintained that his government's achievements in the areas of education, health, and other social services were equally impressive. A mass literacy campaign had made Ghana the most literate country in the whole of Africa, and with nearly 10,000 primary and middle schools, 85 secondary schools, 47 teacher training colleges, 11 technical schools, and 3 universities, Ghana had one of the best educational systems of all the independent states in Africa. The government also undertook public health programs aimed at eliminating common regional diseases such as malaria, lowering the rate of infant mortality, improving nutrition, and instituting preventive health programs. Other state enterprises — agriculture, fish processing and marketing, cattle and poultry

AP/WIDE WORLD PHOTOS

**Students of the College of Administration, one of the many schools founded by Nkrumah's government, welcome Nkrumah's tour of their campus with slogans relating education to the fight against imperialism.**

**By the mid-1960s, Nkrumah's nationwide literacy campaign had made Ghana the most literate country in Africa. Foreign instructors were recruited to supplement the teaching staffs of Ghana's schools.**

farming, timber industries, and rubber production — were greatly modernized under Nkrumah's direction. As he had hoped, the Volta River Project made possible the development of many other industries, due to the increase in available inexpensive electricity it provided.

While Nkrumah's restructuring of Ghana's economy was successful in some respects, it was a failure in many others. The country amassed a huge foreign debt in order to finance many of his industrial and social programs. Under Nkrumah's leadership, foreign exchange reserves of $481 million became a $1 billion national debt. The government was charged with wastefulness when it built a multi-million dollar conference hall to host a single meeting of the Organization of African Unity. Many of the state-owned farms and factories were unprofitable, and the Nkrumah government made many naive financial decisions, such as exchanging cocoa, a popular export, for unpopular goods such as

Bulgarian wine and Soviet canned potatoes. Although Nkrumah had managed to alleviate some of the hunger that plagued most of Africa, Ghana faced severe food shortages during his regime. A sharp drop in the price of cocoa on the world market created additional hardship and further damaged an already unstable economy.

Obviously, there had been some mismanagement and mistakes in Nkrumah's financial strategies, but compared with the record of those who followed him, the economic development plans of his administration were at least relatively successful. Moreover, although charges of corruption against some officials in Nkrumah's government were proven, it has never been proven that Nkrumah himself was corrupt. In his will Nkrumah left all of his belongings to his political party, and at his death in 1972 his British bank account contained only about £10,000 (around $25,000), which he had earned from book sales.

In *Dark Days in Ghana* Nkrumah gives his version of the events that took place after his overthrow. He tells of how the new government dismembered his economic programs: the Seven Year Development Plan was immediately scrapped, and all work on state industries and enterprises was stopped. These enterprises were soon offered for sale to foreign corporations. Yet the National Liberation Council was unable to sell many of Ghana's state enterprises because foreign corporations were wary of investing in what they judged to be a politically unstable country. There was also public opposition to some of the proposed sales. Thus, despite the National Liberation Council's efforts to return to an economy primarily run by private corporations, some of Nkrumah's state enterprises continued to provide the basis for the Ghanaian economy.

Many Western nations applauded Nkrumah's overthrow. While all Soviet, Chinese, and Eastern European technical experts and workers were thrown out of the country and the projects they were working on halted, foreign loans and aid poured in from the West.

*Somewhere down the line, however, he became ambitious, built a cult of personality and ruthlessly used the powers invested in him by his constitution. He developed a strange love for absolute power.*

—COLONEL AKWASI AMANKWA
one of the leaders of the
coup that deposed
Nkrumah

Although the National Liberation Council promised to restore the political liberties that had been curtailed under Nkrumah's regime, it passed laws allowing press censorship and arrested citizens critical of the government without obtaining warrants. Military tribunals tried and imprisoned many people who criticized the government. New laws stipulated that anyone who had held office under Nkrumah's government or been a part of any of his organizations would be ineligible to serve in the government for at least 10 years, unless special exemption was granted. Judges and magistrates considered to be sympathetic to Nkrumah were dismissed.

The National Liberation Council became increasingly unpopular and was not effective at managing social services and the economy. There were cutbacks in education, and many health facilities were shut down. As Nkrumah had been forced to do earlier, the new government instituted austerity programs to help pay interest on foreign debts.

General Joseph Ankrah, first leader of the NLC's military government. Although Ankrah's government promised to stop official corruption, Ankrah himself was forced to resign when he was caught taking a bribe.

After an unsuccessful coup attempt in 1967, the National Liberation Council's leader, General Ankrah, resigned when it was disclosed that he had accepted a bribe from a foreign country. Discontent mounted, and in 1969 the National Liberation Council surrendered power to civilian rule in an election won by one of Nkrumah's former opponents, Dr. K. A. Busia.

Although international agencies and foreign governments provided much aid and emergency loans to the military and civilian governments that followed Nkrumah's, succeeding governments proved themselves incapable of managing the nation's finances. Ghana's economy collapsed under the pressure of growing unemployment and inflation.

Political turmoil was common in Ghana following Nkrumah's ouster. Busia's regime was overthrown by another military government, and since then there has been nearly constant political instability, with civilian and military governments following one another with alarming frequency.

K. A. Busia, center left, greets UN officials in 1969, the year in which he became prime minister after elections restored civilian rule to Ghana. He was soon overthrown by another military government. Constant political turmoil and instability followed Nkrumah's fall from power.

# 10
# Exile, Later Writings, and Death

When Nkrumah learned of his overthrow during his trip to China to discuss the Vietnam War, he immediately sent off a message to the press:

"On my arrival in Peking, my attention has been drawn to reports from press agencies which allege that some members of the Ghana armed forces supported by some members of the police have attempted to overthrow my government — the government of the Convention People's party.

"I know that the Ghanaian people are always loyal to me, the party and the government, and all I expect of everyone at this hour of trial is to remain calm, but firm in determination and resistance.

"Officers and men in the Ghana armed forces who are involved in this attempt, are ordered to return to their barracks and wait for my return.

"I am the constitutional head of the Republic of Ghana, and the supreme commander of the armed forces.

"I am returning to Ghana soon."

Yet Nkrumah was never able to return to Ghana; he remained in exile until his death in 1972. Evidently, he had alienated too many people in his

*At the moment you are being suppressed at the point of guns and bayonets and you are made speechless by these same instruments. But I know that even in silence you are determined and resisting. Be assured that I am standing firm behind you. . . . Very soon I shall be with you again.*
—KWAME NKRUMAH
addressing Ghanaians
via radio broadcast in
March 1966

George Gamal Gorkeh Nkrumah pins a medal for distinguished service on his father in 1965, a year before a coup forced Nkrumah into exile and separated his family.

**Ghanaian army officers interrogate men suspected of loyalty to Nkrumah's government three days after the NLC seized power. The new government's top priority was the consolidation of their authority and the suppression of pro-Nkrumah sentiments.**

*In his lifetime he waged a relentless war against colonialism and racism, and even after his death his spirit will, no doubt, continue to inspire the valiant fighter against these twin enemies of Africa.*

—IGNATIUS ACHEAMPONG
Ghana's leader
from 1972–78, on
Nkrumah's death

country. Many believed that he was corrupt and had destroyed the economy or were too confused to organize and act amid the conflicting reports about his failures and alleged corruption and the repressive environment fostered by the National Liberation Council.

Nkrumah and the advisors who had gone to China with him were invited to come to Guinea by its president, Sékou Touré. Nkrumah and Touré had remained close friends since they had formed the Ghana-Guinea union in 1958. Nkrumah's wife and children left Ghana and went to Egypt, where his wife's family lived. During his final years in exile, Nkrumah felt that his family was safer in Egypt, so he seldom saw them.

When Nkrumah arrived in Guinea in early March he received a warm welcome from the Guinean government and people. At a mass rally in a packed sports stadium in Guinea's capital, Conakry, Touré proclaimed Nkrumah secretary-general of the Guinean Democratic party and co-head of state. Touré had taken the unparalleled step of offering to share power. As Nkrumah later wrote: "Such a gesture of political solidarity must surely be without historical precedent. When our historians come to record the

102

events of 1966 they will doubtless consider the action of the Guinean government as a great landmark in the practical expression of pan-Africanism."

Nkrumah was given a villa on the beach in Conakry and began what he later described as "one of the most fruitful and happiest periods" of his life. Touré visited Nkrumah almost every day to discuss government affairs with him, and Nkrumah received other guests from all over Africa. Nkrumah describes this period in *Dark Days in Ghana*: "I have been able to read as much as I like, to study the latest books on politics, history, literature, science and philosophy, to step up my writing, to reflect, and to prepare myself physically and mentally for the militant phase of the revolutionary struggle."

Nkrumah seemed to focus more than ever on his goal of liberating all of Africa from colonial rule, and he was now convinced that armed struggle was the only viable method. He wrote the *Handbook of Revolutionary Warfare*, published in 1967, and *Class Struggle in Africa*, published in 1970. Nkrumah argued that the 25 successful military coups that had taken place in Africa from 1961 to 1969 — including the one that had driven him from power — were the result of a union between wealthy, ambitious Africans and foreign powers, with the military and police serving as their instruments. Given this situation, Nkrumah argued that only armed strug-

**Sékou Touré, the president of Guinea. He and Nkrumah forged a strong friendship as they worked together for African unity; in 1966 Touré took the unprecedented step of making Nkrumah the co-president of Guinea after the NLC took over the government in Ghana.**

**Touré and Nkrumah at an African summit conference held in 1965, where Nkrumah passionately denounced the white racist government of Rhodesia.**

GHANA

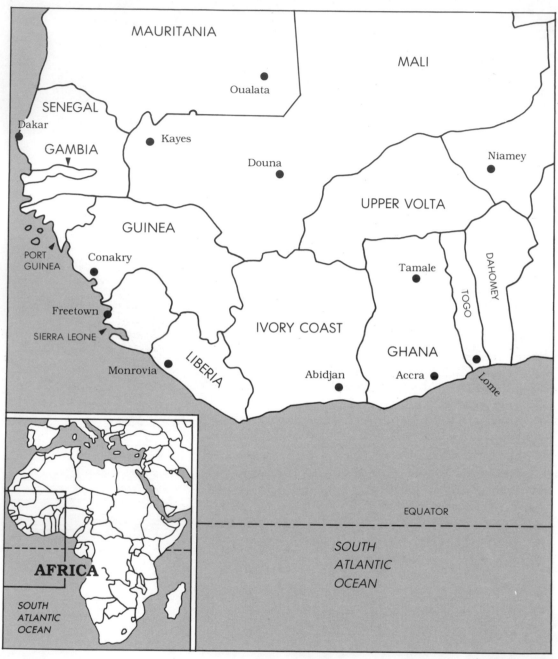

MAURITANIA

MALI

SENEGAL

Oualata

Dakar

GAMBIA

Kayes

Niamey

GUINEA

Douna

UPPER VOLTA

PORT GUINEA

Conakry

DAHOMEY

Tamale

TOGO

Freetown

SIERRA LEONE

IVORY COAST

GHANA

Monrovia

LIBERIA

Abidjan

Accra

Lome

AFRICA

SOUTH ATLANTIC OCEAN

EQUATOR

SOUTH ATLANTIC OCEAN

**Map of West Africa in the mid-1960s showing the locations of Guinea and Ghana. Between March and December of 1966, Nkrumah broadcast speeches into Ghana from Guinea's capital, Conakry, in an attempt to rally his supporters and discredit the new Ghanaian regime.**

gle and guerrilla warfare carried out by African "workers and peasants" could end the colonial domination of the continent and make African democracy possible. Nkrumah had surrendered his earlier belief in nonviolent social change, which he now considered unrealistic.

To the end of his days, Nkrumah remained a defender of armed African revolution and a champion of pan-African union. He believed that only with the liberation and unity of Africa would the continent become a truly independent and viable economic unit. He felt that the African countries were too small, divided, and underdeveloped to industrialize individually and to develop modern economies independently. Instead, he envisioned a United States of Africa, which would share resources and coordinate the economy of the African continent as a whole.

In 1970, while he was still in Guinea, Portugese-backed mercenaries invaded the country and staged an unsuccessful coup. It was at about this time that Nkrumah was stricken with cancer. In 1971 he traveled to Romania to seek treatment, but the disease was too advanced. On April 27, 1972, Nkrumah died in a Romanian hospital. An official funeral service was held in Guinea, and after several months of negotiations, he was finally buried in his home town in Ghana. By this time, yet another new government was in power, one that was sympathetic to Nkrumah. Flags were flown at half-mast when he died and during his funeral, and he was accorded honors reserved for national heroes. When Nkrumah's mother, blind and almost 100 years old, gently laid her hand on Nkrumah's coffin, onlookers could not suppress tears.

African leaders paid emotional tribute to Nkrumah. President Sékou Touré of Guinea stated, "Nkrumah in his lifetime incarnated the struggle of the African peoples against imperialism, colonialism, and neocolonialism. Nkrumah is not dead and could not die. By paying tribute to his memory the Guinean people are expressing fidelity to the ideals of liberty, democracy and progress, which through-

AP/WIDE WORLD PHOTOS

**Nkrumah's longtime friend President Jomo Kenyatta of Kenya (left) and Prime Minister Milton Obote of Uganda in 1964. After Nkrumah's death on April 27, 1972, Kenyatta mourned the passing of a man he characterized as one of Africa's "most dedicated sons."**

*He was the salt that seasoned Ghana and Africa.*
—Nkrumah's mother, at his graveside

Hilla Limann, head of a civilian government that came to power in 1979, equated his role as Ghana's head of state with "sitting on a time bomb." For Limann, the explosion came in 1981 when, like Nkrumah, he was overthrown by a military coup.

out his life underlay the courageous and untiring activities of our brother, friend, and companion-in-arms, President Kwame Nkrumah."

The president of Kenya, Jomo Kenyatta, who had known Nkrumah since the days they had spent together in London in the 1940s, said, "Kwame Nkrumah's death has deprived Africa of one of her most dedicated sons who spearheaded the struggle for liberation and freedom of the continent." The chairman of the Organization for African Unity proclaimed, "The name of our departed brother, Nkrumah, will forever remain enshrined in the annals of African history as one of Africa's most courageous sons. His vital and exemplary contribution

A young Ghanaian woman displays her country's flag. Despite the instability that has characterized national politics, Ghanaians have retained an intense pride in their country, due in large part to Nkrumah's legacy of stalwart anticolonialism and pan-Africanism.

to the liberation and unity of the continent is an honor not only to Ghana but to Africa."

Nkrumah was mourned not just in Africa, but around the world. Even some of his harshest critics had softened. As Robin McKown, one of Nkrumah's most sympathetic biographers wrote: "Nkrumah's prestige had been rising in the years of his exile. The old scandals had died, like overwatered plants, of their own exaggerations. The failures of military dictatorship had aroused more sympathy for Nkrumah and a clearer understanding of the prodigious problems he faced in leading the first nation south of the Sahara to be freed from colonialism. In the tense situation that enveloped Africa as one new nation after another fell victim to plots and counterplots, Nkrumah's stern one-party rule was looked upon with greater tolerance."

The man who was hailed as a "Modern Moses" as he led his people to independence was a complex individual. He relinquished his belief in the effectiveness of nonviolence to advocate armed struggle in the interests of African independence during his last years. Although Nkrumah considered himself a Christian and publicly supported modernization and opposed superstition, in his private life he consulted soothsayers and participated in traditional African tribal rituals. While he was described, even by his critics, as a man of great charm and charisma, he could also be an autocrat who ruthlessly stifled opposition.

In March 1986 the Ghanaian government sponsored a symposium in Accra entitled "Ghana — 20 Years since Nkrumah." Nkrumah was paid tribute as the architect of his country's independence, a champion of black self-awareness, and one of the greatest African leaders of the century. Although he made many mistakes, he is likely to be remembered for his achievements and his visionary ideal of a united Africa. The precise effect that Nkrumah's career will have on the future of African politics will be a story for future historians to tell.

AP/WIDE WORLD PHOTOS

**A statue honoring President Kwame Nkrumah, the founder of the state of Ghana. Nkrumah's ambitious plans and idealism ultimately could not spare his nation the turmoil and hardship that attended Ghana's transition from a dependent colony into a modern nation.**

# Further Reading

Apter, David. *Ghana in Transition.* New York: Atheneum, 1968.

Armah, Kwesi. *Ghana: Nkrumah's Legacy.* London: Rex Collings, 1974.

Bretton, Henry. *The Rise and Fall of Kwame Nkrumah.* New York: Praeger, 1966.

Davidson, Basil. *Africa in History.* New York: Macmillan, 1969.

Fitch, Bob and Mary Oppenheimer. *Ghana: End of an Illusion.* New York: Monthly Review, 1968.

James, C. L. R. *Nkrumah and the Ghana Revolution.* London: Lawrence Hill, 1977.

McKown, Robin. *Nkrumah: A Biography.* Garden City, New York: Doubleday, 1973.

Nkrumah, Kwame. *Africa Must Unite.* New York: International Publishers, 1963.

————. *Class Struggle in Africa.* New York: International Publishers, 1970.

————. *Dark Days in Ghana.* New York: International Publishers, 1968.

————. *Ghana: The Autobiography of Kwame Nkrumah.* New York: International Publishers, 1971.

————. *Handbook of Revolutionary Warfare.* New York: International Publishers, 1967.

————. *Neocolonialism: The Last Stage of Imperialism.* New York: International Publishers, 1965.

————. *Revolutionary Path.* New York: International Publishers, 1973.

Omari, T. Peter. *Kwame Nkrumah, the Anatomy of an African Dictatorship.* New York: Africana, 1970.

Phillips, John. *Kwame Nkrumah and the Future of Africa.* New York: Praeger, 1960.

Stockwell, John. *In Search of Enemies.* New York: Norton, 1978.

Timothy, Bankole. *Kwame Nkrumah from Cradle to Grave.* Dorchester, England: Gavin, 1981.

# Chronology

| | |
|---|---|
| Sept. 1909 | Born Kwame Nkrumah in the British colony of the Gold Coast |
| 1927 | Enters the Government Training College at Accra |
| 1935–43 | Studies in the United States, earning a B.A. in theology and an M.A. in education and philosophy |
| 1945 | Moves to England and becomes involved in the pan-African movement |
| | Becomes increasingly involved with the pan-African movement |
| 1947 | Returns to Africa to become general secretary of the United Gold Coast Convention; is briefly jailed |
| June 12, 1949 | Announces the formation of the Convention People's party |
| 1950 | Nkrumah's "positive action" campaign and a successful general strike lead to his imprisonment |
| Feb. 12, 1951 | British authorities free Nkrumah after his election to the Legislative Assembly; he is appointed leader of government business |
| 1952 | Nkrumah becomes prime minister |
| 1953 | Delivers his "motion of destiny" speech calling for Gold Coast independence |
| March 6, 1957 | The Gold Coast wins independence; is renamed Ghana |
| April 1958 | Ghana hosts the Independent African States conference |
| 1958 | Ghana and Guinea form a political union |
| 1960 | New constitution approved; Nkrumah declared president |
| 1961 | Nkrumah delivers his "dawn broadcast," attacking governmental corruption and defending his administration's socialist policies |
| | Mali joins Ghana and Guinea's political union |
| 1963 | Publication of *Africa Must Unite* |
| | Foundation of Organization of African Unity |
| | Nkrumah marries Fathia Helim Rizik |
| 1964 | Launches a socialist Seven Year Development Plan |
| | One-party state approved in referendum; Nkrumah named "party leader for life" |
| 1965 | Publication of *Neocolonialism: The Last Stage of Imperialism* |
| Feb. 24, 1966 | Nkrumah overthrown in military coup; exiled to Guinea, where he is made co-president |
| 1967 | Publication of *Handbook of Revolutionary Warfare* |
| 1968 | Publication of *Dark Days in Ghana* |
| 1970 | Publication of *Class Struggle in Africa* |
| April 27, 1972 | Dies in Bucharest, Romania, where he was being treated for cancer |
| 1973 | Publication of *Revolutionary Path* |

# Index

Mussolini, Benito, 24
Nasser, Gamal Abdel, 65
National African Socialist Students'
    Association, 75
National Association for the Advancement of
    Colored People (NAACP), 32
National Council of Ghana Women, 75
National Liberation Council, 89, 97, 98, 99,
    102
National Liberation Front (FLN), 58, 61
*Neocolonialism: The Last Stage of
    Imperialism*, 81
*New African, The*, 89
New York, 25, 31
*New York Times, The*, 89
Nigeria, 24, 61
Nkrumah, Kwame
    birth, 21
    colonialism and, 33, 34, 35, 49, 74, 81,
        82, 83
    coup against, 86, 87, 101
    criticism of, 91, 92, 93, 94, 95, 96, 97,
        102
    death, 105
    education, 23, 24, 25, 26
    in exile, 101, 102, 103
    jailed, 16, 37, 44, 45
    leads independence movement, 13, 14,
        16, 37, 39, 40, 42, 43, 44, 49, 53,
        54
    marriage, 65
    modernization of Ghana and, 67, 68,
        71, 95, 96
    Pan-African movement and, 19, 28, 31,
        32, 33, 55, 57, 59, 60, 61, 64, 65, 92,
        103, 105
    political activist, 16, 27, 28, 29, 31, 33
    president of Ghana, 60, 63, 67, 71, 72,
        75, 76, 77, 79, 81
    prime minister, 48, 50, 51, 52
    socialism and, 69, 71–79, 81, 83, 92
    teacher, 24, 26
Oppenheimer, Mary, 68

Organization of African Unity (OAU), 64, 96,
    106
*Osagyefo see* Nkrumah, Kwame
Oxford University, 31
Padmore, George, 31
Pan-African Conference, 31, 32
Pennsylvania, 24
Pennsylvania, University of, 26, 27
Philadelphia, 47
*Philosophy and Opinions of Marcus Garvey*
    (Garvey), 29
Plato, 26
Portugal, 16
Presidential Guard Unit, 86
Rhodesia (Zimbabwe), 59, 85, 86
Rizik, Fathia Helim (wife), 65
Romania, 105
Sahara Desert, 15, 63
Seven Year Development Plan, 77, 78, 97
South Africa, 59, 64
South West Africa, 64
Soviet Union, 63, 71, 72, 81
Stockwell, John, 88
Takoradi, 67, 95
Tema, 95
Togo, 52, 61
Touré, Sékou, 102, 103, 105
"Toward Colonial Freedom," 33
Trades Union Congress, 43, 74
Union of African States, 59, 60
United Ghana Farmers' Council, 74
United Gold Coast Convention (UGCC), 35,
    37, 39, 40, 41
United Nations, 47
United States, 16, 24, 25, 26, 27, 29, 31,
    32, 42, 47, 81
Vietnam, 86
Volta River Project, 79, 95, 96
West Africa, 21, 35
West African National Secretariat, 35
West African Students' Union, 31
Winneba, 75
World War II, 36, 82

**Douglas Kellner** is Professor of Philosophy at the University of Texas at Austin and is the author of *Karl Korsch: Revolutionary Theory, Herbert Marcuse and the Crisis of Marxism* and co-author of *Camera Politica: The Politics and Ideology of Contemporary Hollywood Film.* He is currently at work on a book on critical theory and a biography of Jean Baudrillard.

---

**Arthur M. Schlesinger, jr.,** taught history at Harvard for many years and is currently Albert Schweitzer Professor of the Humanities at City University of New York. He is the author of numerous highly praised works in American history and has twice been awarded the Pulitzer Prize. He served in the White House as special assistant to Presidents Kennedy and Johnson.